Scrapbooking
With
cricut™

Edited by **Tanya Fox**

Annie's Attic®

Scrapbooking With Cricut™

EDITOR Tanya Fox

ART DIRECTOR Brad Snow

PUBLISHING SERVICES DIRECTOR Brenda Gallmeyer

ASSOCIATE EDITOR Brooke Smith

ASSISTANT ART DIRECTOR Nick Pierce

COPY SUPERVISOR Michelle Beck

COPY EDITORS Emily Carter, Amanda Scheerer

TECHNICAL EDITOR Corene Painter

PHOTOGRAPHY SUPERVISOR Tammy Christian

PHOTO STYLISTS Tammy Liechty, Tammy Steiner

PHOTOGRAPHY Matthew Owen

PRODUCTION ARTIST SUPERVISOR Erin Augsburger

GRAPHIC ARTIST Nicole Gage

PRODUCTION ASSISTANSTS Marj Morgan,
    Judy Neuenschwander

Printed in the United States of America
First Printing: 2010
ISBN: 978-1-59635-323-7
1 2 3 4 5 6 7 8 9

Contents

Happy New Year

Celebrate with family and friends as you ring in the New Year!

Design by **Kimber McGray**

Use a 12 x 12-inch sheet of embossed card stock as layout base.

Using Plantin SchoolBook cartridge and black card stock, cut a 6-inch "2010" by pressing "<2>," "<0>," "<1>" and "<0>." Cut a 1¾-inch scallop border by pressing "<scallop>."

Using Sweet Treats cartridge and yellow card stock, cut a 3-inch party favor by pressing "<favor>." Repeat with red and black card stock.

Using Wild Card cartridge and red card stock, cut a 10-inch "Happy New Year." Select Phrase feature and press "<celbrat>."

Adhere "2010" to top of layout page. Adhere scallop 4 inches below "2010". Cut two 4 x 4-inch squares from white card stock. These will be the photo mats. Adhere to layout as shown. Adhere photos to photo mats.

Trim small curl off red party favor; adhere to yellow party favor. Trim medium curl off black party favor; adhere to yellow party favor. Use marker to ink edges of yellow party favor. Adhere layered party favor to layout as shown. Adhere "Happy New Year" over "2010" as shown. ●

Sources: Card stock and embossed card stock from Core'dinations; Cricut machine and cartridges from Provo Craft.

Skill level
Easy

Materials
- Cricut Expression machine
- Cartridges:
  Plantin SchoolBook (#29-0390),
  Sweet Treats (#29-1557),
  Wild Card (#29-0591)
- Card stock: red, yellow, black
- Jillibean Soup Numbers Tranquil Blue embossed card stock
- Black fine-tip marker
- Paper adhesive

Let It Snow

Celebrate the fun of wintery snow-covered days
with this bright and colorful layout.

Design by **Lynn Ghahary**

Use two 12 x 12-inch sheets of aqua card stock for layout base.

Adhere a 12 x 5-inch piece of green snowflake paper 1 inch from top on each side of layout base. Adhere a 12 x ½-inch piece of striped paper on top edge of green snowflake paper on each side of layout base as shown.

Cut an 8½ x 11-inch piece of pink dot paper; round lower left and lower right corners. Referring to photo, cut piece vertically 1⅛ inches from right edge. Adhere large piece to left page of layout flush with top and inside edges. Adhere small piece to right page of layout flush to inside and top edges. Adhere photos to layout as represented by white photo rectangles.

Cut a 12 x ½-inch piece of striped paper. Cut into two pieces 5¾ inches from left edge. Adhere 12 x 5¾-inch strip to left page of layout along bottom edge of photos as shown. Adhere remaining strip to bottom edge of photos on right page of layout as shown, aligning strips.

Using Winter Wonderland cartridge and white glitter card stock, cut a 3½-inch "Let It Snow" by pressing "<LetItSnw>." Repeat with green and light blue card stock. Cut a base in the same manner from brown card stock; press "<shift>" and "<LetItSnw>."

Cut a 3-inch scalloped circle from green card stock by selecting Shadow/Blackout feature. Press "<shift>" and "<Snowflk1>." Repeat once. Cut a 3-inch circle from brown card stock by pressing "<shift>" and "<Snowflk1>." Repeat once. Cut a 3-inch snowflake from white glitter card stock by selecting Layers feature. Press "<Snowflk4>." Repeat once.

Adhere green "Let It," white "Snow" and blue snowflakes to "Let It Snow" brown base. Using dimensional adhesive, attach to layout as shown.

Adhere brown circles to green scalloped circles. Adhere to layout as shown. Using dimensional adhesive, attach snowflakes to layered circles. ●

Source: Cricut machine and cartridge from Provo Craft.

Skill level
Easy

Materials
- Cricut Expression machine
- Cartridge: Winter Woodland (#29-1046)
- Card stock: white glitter, aqua, brown, light blue
- Printed papers: green snowflake, pink dot, multicolored striped
- Black fine-tip marker
- Corner rounder
- Dimensional adhesive
- Paper adhesive

Snow

Create this gorgeous Snow Day layout for those crisp, first snowfall of the year memories!

Design by **Joy Tracey**

Use a 12 x 12-inch sheet of Redwood Hideaway paper as layout base. Adhere an 11½ x 11½-inch square of Flurry Kisses paper centered to layout base.

Cut a 12 x 3-inch strip of white glitter card stock; tear in half horizontally. Using Cuttlebug embossing machine and D'vine Swirls embossing folder, emboss both pieces of white glitter card stock. Adhere to bottom of layout as shown.

Cut a 6½ x 4½-inch rectangle of Winter Song paper; adhere to red card stock; trim a small border. Adhere layered rectangle to My Wooly Scarf paper; trim a small border. Adhere a photo to layered rectangle. Wrap an 8½-inch length of red velvet ribbon across top of layered rectangle; secure ends to back. Adhere to top right corner of layout as shown. Decorate with a snowflake and rhinestone.

In the same manner as in previous paragraph, create a second photo spot by repeating layering process with a 4¼ x 4¾-inch piece of Winter Song paper, red card stock and My Wooly Scarf paper. Embellish with red velvet ribbon, snowflake and rhinestone as shown.

Using Winter Woodland cartridge and pink card stock, cut an 8-inch building by pressing "<Bldg1>." Using red striped card stock, repeat cut pressing "<shift>" first. Cut an 8-inch building layer from Crystal Arabesque paper by selecting Layer feature, press "<Bdg1>." Using white glitter card stock, repeat cut pressing "<shift>" first.

Cut a 2½-inch "Snow" oval from white glitter card stock by selecting Tag feature; press "<SnowDay>." Using red fabric paper, repeat cut pressing "<shift>" first.

Cut a 2¾-inch journaling tag from My Wooly Scarf paper by selecting Tag feature; press "<shift>" and "<Cap>." Repeat cut at 2½-inch setting using blue card stock.

Assemble and adhere building layers as shown. Adhere to lower left corner of layout. String white twine through pink button; tie knot and trim ends. Adhere to building as shown.

Adhere white "Snow" over red layer. Pierce holes on right and left edges and insert red glitter brads. Using foam dots, attach between photo rectangles.

Stamp journaling lines onto blue tag; adhere to striped tag. Adhere to layout above building. Tie white twine through red button; tie knot and trim ends; adhere to remaining snowflake. Attach to journaling tag. ●

Skill level
Easy

Materials
- Cricut Expression machine
- Cartridge:
  Winter Woodland (#29-1046)
- Cuttlebug machine
- Embossing folder:
  D'vine Swirls (#37-1142)
- Card stock: red, blue, pink, red striped, white glitter
- Winter Song printed papers:
  My Wooly Scarf Foil, Redwood Hideaway, Crystal Arabesque Foil, Winter Song Flocked, Flurry Kisses
- Red fabric printed paper
- Annotations stamp set
- Red ink pad
- 15 inches ⅝-inch-wide red velvet ribbon
- Buttons: 1 pink, 1 red
- White twine
- 3 clear plastic snowflakes
- 2 clear rhinestones
- 2 red glitter brads
- Piercing tool
- Adhesive foam dots
- Paper adhesive

Sources: Card stock and printed papers from SEI; stamp set from Close To My Heart; snowflakes from Heidi Swapp; brads from Making Memories; Cricut machine and cartridge, Cuttlebug machine and embossing folder from Provo Craft.

Be Mine

Showcase your favorite Valentine's Day photos on this fun layout featuring an easy-to-make, paper-hearts ribbon.

Design by **Summer Fullerton**

Skill level
Easy

Materials
- Cricut Expression machine
- Cartridges:
  Doodletype (#29-0054),
  Opposites Attract (#29-0227)
- Card stock: kraft, black, mauve
- Printed papers: assorted pink, red
- Cupid die-cut tag
- Black fine-tip marker
- Buttons: assorted pink, red
- 62 inches ¼-inch-wide pink grosgrain ribbon
- 4 black heart brads
- Piercing tool
- Tape
- Adhesive foam squares
- Paper adhesive

Use two 12 x 12-inch sheets of kraft card stock as layout base. Lay two sheets of mauve card stock side by side. Referring to photo, draw a wavy line along top of pages; cut along wavy line. Adhere to layout base aligning bottom edges.

Using Doodletype cartridge and assorted printed papers, cut 24 (1¾-inch) hearts by pressing "<shift>" and "<8>."

Using Opposites Attract cartridge and black card stock, cut a 2-inch "BE MINE" by selecting Opposite feature. Press "<Shift Lock>," "<b>," "<e>," "<m>," "<i>," "<n>" and"<e>." Repeat cut using Opposite Shadow feature.

Cut six 4½-inch heart stick pins, two each from three different printed papers by pressing "<shift>" and "<stickpin>."

Cut a 1-inch "xo xo xo" from black card stock by using Opposites feature. Press "<x>," "<o>," "<x>," "<o>," "<x>" and "<o>." Repeat cut using Opposite Shadow feature.

Adhere hearts along wavy border overlapping them as shown. Adhere buttons to extra hearts. Using foam squares, layer extra hearts over border hearts as desired.

Adhere photos to layout as as represented by white photo rectangles; trim if needed. Using foam squares, layer heart stick pins to matching stick pins. Referring to photo, adhere stick pins to layout.

Referring to photo, wrap two 13-inch pieces of ribbon around left page, securing ends on back of page with tape. In the same manner, wrap a 13-inch piece of ribbon around right page. Cut remaining ribbon in half; secure one end of each piece to back of right layout page above previous ribbon as shown. String tag onto one side of ribbon and tie a bow over stick pins as shown. Trim ends.

Adhere "BE MINE" to its shadow. Using foam squares, attach words to page as shown. Add black heart brads using piercing tool to pierce holes.

In the same manner, adhere "xo xo xo" to its shadow and attach over ribbon on lower right area of page. ●

Sources: Card stock from Bazzill Basics Paper Inc.; printed papers from Making Memories, Jenni Bowlin Studio, Jillibean Soup and Pink Paislee; die-cut tag from Pink Paislee; Cricut machine and cartridges from Provo Craft.

Make a Wish...

Birthday wishes really will come true with this fun layout!

Design by **Shirlene Jordan**

Use a 12 x 12-inch sheet of multicolored circles paper for left layout page base. Round corners of an 11½ x 11½ piece of green printed paper; center and adhere to left layout page.

Use a 12 x 12-inch sheet of lime green printed paper for right layout page base. Adhere a 12 x 4-inch piece of multicolored floral paper 1⅛ inches from bottom of right layout page. Round corners of an 11 x 3½-inch piece of cream lined paper; ink edges brown. Adhere to right layout page as shown.

Using Sweet Treats cartridge and pink dot paper, cut a 4½-inch cake by selecting "<Cake4>."

Cut a 4½-inch "Happy Birthday" from brown card stock by selecting Layers feature; press "<Cake4>." In the same manner, cut frosting layers from dark pink card stock by selecting Layers feature; press "<shift>" and "<Cake4>."

Cut a 1¾-inch "2" candle from dark pink card stock by pressing "<2>." In the same manner, cut a top layer "2" from white dot paper by pressing "<shift>" first. Cut a 2-inch flame for candle from lime green printed paper by selecting Layers feature; press "<shift>" and "<2>."

Cut a 2¾-inch cake plate from white dot paper by pressing "<CakePlte>." Using same paper, repeat cut pressing Shadow/Blackout feature first.

Cut a 7-inch photo tag from pink printed paper by selecting Tag feature; press "<Flower1>." In the same manner, cut top layer from dark pink printed paper by pressing "<shift>" first.

Cut a 3-inch "Make a Wish" title from lime green printed card stock by pressing "<MakeAWish>." In the same manner, cut title shadow from brown printed paper by selecting Shadow/Blackout feature first.

Cut a 2-inch flower from dark pink card stock and pressing "<Flower1>." In the same manner, repeat cut using pink printed paper and pressing "<shift>" first. Repeat cut using same paper. Cut final layer for 2-inch flower from lime green card stock by selecting Layers feature; press "<Flower1>."

Cut a 2¼-inch flower from lime green card stock by pressing "<Flower2>." In the same manner, repeat cut using dark pink card stock and pressing "<shift>" first. Repeat cut using white dot paper. Cut final layer of 2¼-inch flower from brown printed paper by selecting Layers feature; press "<Flower2>."

Cut a 2½-inch flower from lime green card stock by pressing "<Flower3>." In the same manner, cut second flower layer from dark pink card stock by pressing "<shift>" first. Repeat cut using pink printed paper. Cut final layer of 2½-inch flower from brown printed paper by selecting Layers feature; press "<Flower3>."

Cut a 2¼-inch flower from dark pink card stock by pressing "<Flower 4>." Repeat to cut second flower layer using hot pink printed paper at 2-inch setting. Cut final layer of flower from brown printed paper at 2-inch setting by selecting Layers feature; press "<Flower4>."

Skill level
Intermediate

Materials
- Cricut Expression machine
- Cartridges:
  Sweet Treats (#29-1557),
  A Child's Year (#29-0833)
- Card stock: brown, dark pink, pink, lime green printed
- Printed papers: multicolored circles, pink dot, white dot, cream lined, dark pink, pink, lime green, green, brown, multicolored floral
- Brown ink pad
- Brown string
- Corner rounder
- Paper adhesive

Cut a 2½-inch flower from pink printed paper by pressing "<Flower5>." Repeat cut using white dot paper and pressing "<shift>" first. Repeat cut using lime green printed card stock. Cut final layer for 2½-inch flower from dark pink printed paper by selecting Layers feature and pressing "<Flower5>."

Cut a 3½-inch flower from pink dot paper by pressing "<Flower1>." In the same manner, repeat cut using dark pink card stock by pressing "<shift>" first. Repeat cut using pink card stock. Cut final layer for 3½-inch flower from lime green card stock by selecting Layers feature; press "<Flower1>."

Cut a 7-inch present from dark pink printed paper by pressing "<Presnt2>." Repeat cut using pink printed paper by pressing "<shift>" first.

Cut a 7-inch present from dark pink card stock by pressing "<Prsnt1>." In the same manner, cut present lid from multicolored floral paper by pressing "<shift>" first.

Cut a 3-inch tag from pink printed paper by selecting Tag feature; press "<Hat3>." In the same manner, cut tag top from white dot paper by pressing "<shift>" first. Cut a 2¼-inch "2" from brown card stock by pressing "<shift> and "<2>."

Using A Child's Year cartridge, cut a 7-inch child in highchair from brown card stock by selecting Flip feature; press "<Birthday1>."

Ink edges of all flower layers, lime green "Make A Wish" title, cake plate layers, present layers and top of tags brown. Assemble and adhere flower layers together as shown. Adhere largest flower to upper right corner of cream lined rectangle on right page of layout. Adhere remaining five flowers to lower left corner of left layout page.

Adhere cake plate layers together and adhere to layout above five flowers.

Adhere "happy birthday" to center of cake; place cake above cake plate on layout. Adhere layered "2" candle to top of cake. Adhere frosting layers to cake as shown.

Adhere lime green "Make A Wish" title to its brown shadow. Adhere to left layout page as shown.

Adhere dark pink tag top to pink tag; adhere to layout as shown.

Assemble and adhere layers of presents together. Adhere to layout as shown.

Adhere brown "2" to pink printed paper tag. Adhere white dot tag top to tag. Hold two 5-inch lengths of string together and fold in half; insert folded end through tag hole from back to front; thread unfolded ends of string through formed loop and pull to secure string to tag. Adhere tag to layout as shown. Adhere child in high chair to upper right corner of right layout page. ●

Source: Cricut machine and cartridges from Provo Craft.

Spring Fever

Showcase early spring colors and family fun!

Design by **Georgina Jarvie**

Use two 12 x 12-inch sheets of yellow card stock as layout base. Cut two 11¾ x 11¾ squares of red card stock; adhere to yellow card-stock bases. Cut two 11½ x 11½-inch squares of tan card stock; adhere to red squares.

Using Graphically Speaking cartridge and striped card stock, cut a 10½-inch tree. Press "<shift>" and "<Imag01>." Repeat with yellow card stock.

Using Wild Card cartridge and tan card stock, cut a 1¼-inch bird on stem. Select Frame feature, press "<shift>" and "<Tweety>." Repeat once using blue printed card stock.

Using yellow card stock, cut a 1½-inch bird by selecting Icon feature and pressing "<Tweety>."

Using yellow card stock, cut a 1¼-inch bird by selecting Icon feature and pressing "<Tweety>." Repeat with blue printed card stock.

Using red printed card stock, cut a 1-inch bird by selecting Icon feature and pressing "<Tweety>."

Using blue printed card stock, cut a 1½-inch bird by selecting Icon feature; press "<shift>" and "<Tweety>." Repeat with red printed card stock.

Skill level
Easy

Materials
- Cricut Expression machine
- Cartridges:
  Graphically Speaking (#29-0590),
  Wild Card (#29-0591),
  Jubliee (#29-0706)
- Cuttlebug machine
- Embossing folder:
  Perfectly Paisley (#37-1619)
- Card stock: yellow, red, green, tan
- Coordinating printed card stock:
  2 spring-themed, striped,
  red, blue
- Brown ink pad
- Blue self-adhesive pearls: 11 small,
  10 medium, 6 large, 5 X-large
- Craft sponge
- Adhesive foam squares
- Paper adhesive

Using yellow card stock, cut a 1¼-inch bird by selecting Icon feature; press "<shift>" and "<Tweety>." Repeat with red printed card stock.

Using yellow card stock, cut a 1-inch bird by selecting Icon feature; press "<shift>" and "<Tweety>."

Using Jubilee cartridge and tan card stock, cut a 2-inch "SPRING FEVER" title. Select Base feature; press "<Shift Lock>" and "<s>," "<p>," "<r>," "<i>," "<n>," "<g>," "<f>," "<e>," "<v>," "<e>" and "<r>." Repeat cut using Shadow feature with yellow card stock and striped card stock.

Cut two 11½ x 1½-inch strips of red printed card stock. Cut two 11½ x 3-inch strips of first spring-themed card stock. Ink edges and layer red strips over spring strips. Adhere to center of each layout base. Attach three small pearls to outside edges of red strips.

Cut two 4⅝ x 5-inch rectangles from second spring-themed card stock. Cut two 4¼ x 4¾-inch rectangles from green card stock. Cut two 4 x 4½-inch rectangles from tan card stock. Sponge ink onto Perfectly Paisley embossing folder and use Cuttlebug and inked folder to emboss tan rectangles. Ink edges of all rectangles and layer together as shown. Referring to photo, adhere two layered rectangles to right page.

Cut a 5 x 7¼-inch rectangle from second spring-themed card stock. Cut a 4½ x 6¾-inch rectangle from green card stock. Cut a 4 x 5-inch rectangle from tan card stock. Using Cuttlebug and inked embossing folder, emboss tan rectangle. Ink edges of all rectangles; layer and adhere together as shown, leaving space at bottom of green rectangle for a bird. Referring to layout, adhere to left page.

Adhere striped tree offset over yellow tree. Cut tree in half about ¾ inch from left side of trunk. Adhere tree with trunk to right page of layout with trimmed edge of branches lined up with left edge of page. Adhere remaining tree branches to left page of layout with trimmed edge lined up to right edge of page.

Using Cuttlebug and inked embossing folder, emboss tan "SPRING FEVER." Adhere yellow shadow "SPRING FEVER" offset over striped shadow. Adhere tan lettering over yellow shadow. Adhere to layout as shown.

Ink edges of tan branch and blue bird. Cut blue bird off its branch and glue to tan bird. Adhere to space at bottom of green rectangle on left page.

Ink edges of all remaining birds and adhere to layout with foam squares in sections shown.

Attach medium pearls to corners of all three embossed rectangles. Attach remaining pearls to tree as desired. ●

Source: Cricut machine and cartridges, Cuttlebug machine and embossing folder from Provo Craft.

Lucky Day

Share your St. Patrick's Day story with this creative and colorful layout.

Design by **Kimber McGray**

Use a 12 x 12-inch sheet of printed paper as layout base.

Using Home Decor cartridge and white card stock, cut a 3-inch large cloud. Select Shadow feature and press "<French Label>." Cut two 2-inch small clouds from white card stock, by selecting Shadow feature and pressing "<French Label>."

Using Plantin SchoolBook cartridge and green card stock, cut a 1¾-inch grass border. Press "<shift>" and "<city>." Repeat.

Cut a 10¾-inch rainbow layer from red card stock by selecting Italic feature; press "<shift>" and "<brace>." Press "<stop>" after first bracket has been cut. Repeat with orange, yellow, green, blue and purple card stocks.

Cut four 1-inch hearts from green card stock to create large shamrock. Select Roly Poly feature and press "<heart>." In the same manner, cut eight hearts at ½-inch setting and four at ¼-inch setting.

Cut 1½-inch "Lucky day" from black card stock by pressing "<u>," "<c>," "<k>," "<y>," "<d>," "<a>" and "<y>." Press "<shift>" and "<L>."

Adhere photos to layout as represented by white photo rectangles. Adhere pieces of rainbow together. Adhere to layout with base of rainbow lining up with lower right edge of right photograph.

Cut one grass border into two pieces. Adhere a piece to each side of layout as shown. Adhere remaining grass border centered over previous borders.

Cut a ½ x 11-inch journaling strip of white card stock; adhere below grass border with a short edge lined up with right side of layout.

Assemble four shamrocks with green hearts. Using foam squares, attach large shamrock and two medium shamrocks to rainbow. Adhere small shamrock to right side of journaling strip.

Referring to photo, use foam squares to attach small clouds. Adhere "Lucky day" to large cloud as shown. Using foam squares, attach large cloud to layout over beginning of rainbow. ●

Skill Level
Easy

Materials
- Cricut Expression machine
- Cartridges:
  Home Decor (#29-0695),
  Plantin SchoolBook (#29-0390)
- Card stock: white, red, yellow, orange, blue, green, purple, black
- Soup Staples Light Blue Sugar printed paper
- Black fine-tip marker
- Adhesive foam squares
- Paper adhesive

Sources: Card stock from Core'dinations; printed paper from Jillibean Soup; Cricut machine and cartridges from Provo Craft.

Welcome Baby

It's a banner day when you welcome a new baby into the world!

Design by **Kimber McGray**

Use a 12 x 12-inch sheet of Yellow Sugar paper as layout base.

Using Accent Essentials cartridge and white card stock, cut an 11-inch scallop square by pressing "<shift>"and "<Accent47>."

Using Sweet Treats cartridge and pink, blue and green card stock, cut 2-inch triangles by pressing "<shift>" and "<Hat2>." Repeat four times for each color.

Using Lyrical Letters cartridge and white card stock, cut 1½-inch "welcome baby" by selecting Jack Sprat feature. Press "<w>," "<e>," "<l>," "<c>," "<o>," "<m>," "<e>," "<b>," "<a>," "<b>" and "<y>."

Using Doodlecharms cartridge and yellow card stock, cut a 3¼-inch ducky by pressing "<ducky>." Repeat cut using gray card stock, selecting Shadow feature first.

Stitch a double-square border with white thread on white scallop square; adhere to layout as shown.

Cut two 4 x 6-inch rectangles from green card stock. Adhere photos to rectangles. Adhere rectangles to layout as shown.

Adhere "welcome baby" letters to individual triangles. **Note:** *Trim "l," "b," "b" and "y" to allow them to fit on triangles.* Punch holes in upper corners of triangles; string together with white embroidery floss.

Using foam squares, attach "welcome baby" triangles to layout. Adhere ducky to shadow. Adhere to layout as shown.

Sting floss through a button; tie bow. String floss through remaining buttons; tie knot. Attach three buttons to layout as shown. ●

Sources: Card stock from Core'dinations; printed paper from Jillibean Soup; Cricut machine and cartridges from Provo Craft.

Our Baby

Capture precious moments with your sweet new baby with this quick-to-create page!

Design by **Kandis Smith**

Skill Level
Easy

Materials

- Cricut Expression machine
- Cartridges:
  Plantin SchoolBook (#29-0390),
  Walk in My Garden (#29-0223)
- Cuttlebug machine
- Embossing folder:
  Argyle (#37-1603)
- Card stock: pink, aqua, light aqua,
  yellow, white, kraft
- Quite Contrary Jack & Jill Favorite
  Thing Colorful Umbrellas double-
  sided printed paper
- File folder
- Stamps: scalloped edge,
  Anytime Messages set
- Brown ink pad
- Brown vinyl alphabet stickers
- 2 light brown photo corners
- 8 buttons: pink, white,
  clear, yellow
- Clear self-adhesive rhinestones
- 91 inches cream linen string
- Sewing machine with light
  brown thread
- Adhesive foam squares
- Paper adhesive

Use a 12 x 12-inch sheet of aqua card stock as layout base. Machine-stitch along top and bottom edges of an 8½ x 2-inch piece of printed paper on yellow dot side. Cut an 8½ x 1-inch piece of kraft card stock. Stamp one long edge with scalloped border. Adhere to yellow dot piece as shown.

Adhere layered piece to an 8½ x 11-inch piece of pink card stock as shown. Wrap a piece of linen string around kraft card-stock section. Tie a bow. Adhere layered panel to layout base as shown.

Cut a 3 x 4-inch piece of white card stock; adhere photo corners to top two corners. Cut a 2½ x 3-inch piece of white card stock. Attach white rectangles to layout as shown, using foam squares as desired. Adhere photographs to white rectangles.

Using Cuttlebug and Argyle embossing folder, emboss an 8½ x 5½-inch rectangle of white card stock. Using Plantin SchoolBook cartridge, cut a 3-inch circle from embossed rectangle by pressing "<circle>." In the same manner, moving position of cut with Blade Navigation Buttons, cut two circles using same embossed rectangle at 2-inch setting and one circle at 2½-inch setting.

Cut two 1½-inch circles from white card stock by pressing "<circle>." Cut a 2-inch "baby" title from light aqua card stock by pressing "<b>," "<a>," "<b>" and "<y>."

Using both Plantin SchoolBook and Walk in My Garden cartridges, cut a variety of eight flowers at 1½-inch, 2-inch and 3-inch settings using light aqua and yellow card stock.

Using foam squares, attach embossed rectangle to an 8½ x 5½-inch piece of white card stock.

Tie linen string through buttons, tying bows as desired; adhere to flowers. Adhere a flower to each 1½-inch white card-stock circle. Adhere all flowers to layout as shown, using foam squares as desired. Adhere "baby" title to layout as shown. Above "baby," attach brown stickers spelling "Our."

Using a file folder as a template, cut a tab using kraft card stock; stamp with sentiment, adhere to layout as shown. Add rhinestones to page as desired. ●

Sources: Printed paper from My Mind's Eye; stamp set from Hero Arts; alphabet stickers from American Crafts Inc.; Cricut machine and cartridges, Cuttlebug machine and embossing folder from Provo Craft.

Whimsical New Baby

Capture the fun and excitement of a new addition to the family on this page designed with eye-catching colors and whimsical animal motifs.

Design by **Maggie Lamarre**

Use a 12 x 12-inch piece of blue card stock as layout base.

Cut a 12 x 4½-inch piece of orange printed paper. Punch both long edges with scallop punch; ink edges with markers. Cut a 12 x 5½-inch piece of animal printed paper; punch one long edge with scallop punch; ink edges with markers. Stitch papers together as shown; secure floss ends on back with tape; adhere to layout base as shown.

Cut a 12 x ¼-inch strip and a 12 x ¾-inch strip of orange printed paper. Adhere strips to bottom of layout as shown. Cut a 7 x 5½-inch piece of blue printed paper; adhere to layout as shown. Add photos.

Using Plantin SchoolBook cartridge and orange printed paper, cut a 4-inch "Baby" title by pressing "<shift>," "<b>," "<a>," "<b>" and "<y>."

Using Create a Critter cartridge and orange printed paper, cut a 6½-inch giraffe by pressing "<Giraffe>." Repeat cut using blue card stock, selecting Shadow feature first. Repeat both cuts at 3-inch setting.

Using Straight from the Nest cartridge and animal printed paper, cut a 2-inch photo corner by selecting Corner feature; press "<CakeStnd>."

Using Disney Hannah Montana cartridge and white card stock, cut a 3-inch decorative frame by pressing "<Frame>."

Ink edges of all cut pieces with markers.

Assemble and adhere layers of both giraffes as shown. Decorate giraffes with acrylic stones. Using foam dots, attach giraffes to layout as shown.

Using Cuttlebug and embossing folder, emboss "Baby" title. Wrap a piece of embroidery floss around "y" and tie a knot. Adhere "Baby" to layout as shown. Adhere photo corner to upper right corner of blue rectangle.

Adhere decorative frame to layout next to "B" in baby.

Stamp journaling lines onto white card stock. Trim to 2⅝ x 1¼ inches; round corners. Using foam dots, attach to decorative frame. ●

Sources: Card stock from Core'dinations; paper pad from K&Company; stamp from Technique Tuesday; Double Scallop Edger Punch from Martha Stewart Crafts; Cricut machine and cartridges, Cuttlebug machine and embossing folder from Provo Craft.

Skill level
Intermediate

Materials
- Cricut Expression machine
- Cartridges:
  Plantin SchoolBook (#29-0390), Create a Critter (#2000099), Straight from the Nest (#2000190), Disney Hannah Montana (#29-0702)
- Cuttlebug machine
- Embossing folder: Swiss Dots (#37-1604)
- Card stock: white, blue
- Lion Sleeps Paper Pad
- Journaling stamp
- Black ink pad
- Markers
- Clear acrylic flat-back stones
- Orange embroidery floss
- Sewing needle
- Punches: Double Scallop Edger, corner rounder
- Tape
- Adhesive foam dots
- Paper adhesive

Happy Easter

Feature photos of your favorite Easter moment,
surrounded by charming creatures and fresh spring colors!

Design by **Miranda Urry**

Use two 12 x 12-inch sheets of yellow card stock as layout base. Ink edges light brown. Adhere an 11¼ x 11¼-inch piece of blue checked paper centered to left layout page. Adhere an 11¼ x 11¼-inch piece of pink dot paper centered to right layout page. Adhere a sheet of crest-shaped paper to each layout page as shown.

Cut a 6 x 4-inch rectangle of floral paper; adhere to light blue card stock; trim a border. Using foam squares, attach layered rectangle to brown card stock; trim border. Adhere layered rectangle to right page of layout as shown. Adhere photo to top layer.

Using Easter Seasonal cartridge, cut a 7¾-inch grass from green card stock by pressing "<grass>." Repeat cut. In the same manner, using green printed paper, repeat cut pressing Flip feature first. Repeat cut.

Cut a 6½-inch scalloped egg from brown card stock; press "<Egg1shadow>." Repeat cut using floral paper at 6-inch setting.

Cut a 4-inch sitting bunny from yellow card stock by selecting Flip feature; press "<Bunny5Shadow>." In the same manner, cut top layer from light pink card stock by selecting Flip feature; press "<Bunny5>."

Cut a 6-inch standing bunny from yellow card stock by pressing "<Bunny6Shadow>." In the same manner, cut top layer from light pink card stock by pressing "<Bunny6>."

Cut a 1½-inch chick from yellow card stock by pressing "<chick2>." Repeat cut at 2-inch, 2½-inch and 3½-inch settings.

Cut a 1½-inch bow from light pink card stock by pressing "<ChickLyr2>." Repeat cut using pink card stock. Repeat cuts at 2-inch and 3½-inch settings. Repeat cuts using blue and light blue card stocks at 2½-inch setting.

Cut a 2-inch flower from brown card stock by pressing "<Flwr4Shadow>." Repeat cut, pressing Flip feature. In the same manner, cut top layer of flower from yellow card stock by pressing "<Flower4>." Repeat cut using light blue card stock by selecting Flip Feature first.

Cut a second set of 2-inch flowers from brown card stock by pressing "<Flwr3Shadow>." Repeat cut pressing Flip feature first. In the same manner, cut top layer of flower from yellow card stock by pressing "<Flower3>." Repeat cut using pink card stock by selecting Flip feature first.

Skill Level
Intermediate

Materials
- Cricut Expression machine
- Cartridge:
  Easter Seasonal (#2000100)
- Card stock: yellow, light pink,
  pink, light blue, blue,
  brown, green
- Printed papers: green, floral, blue
  checked, pink dot, pink crest-
  shaped, blue/green crest-shaped
- Ink pads: light brown, blue, pink
- 10 inches ¾-inch-wide blue
  ribbon
- 6 gems in corresponding colors
  and sizes
- Adhesive foam squares
- Paper adhesive

Cut a 2-inch "Happy Easter" title from brown card stock by pressing "<HappyEasterShadow>." In the same manner, cut top layer of title from yellow card stock by pressing "<HappyEaster>."

Cut three 2-inch eggs from brown card stock by pressing "<Egg2Shadow>." In the same manner, cut egg top layer from light blue card stock by pressing "<Egg2>." Repeat top layer cut using light pink and yellow card stock.

Cut 1 inch off bottom of each grass border. Using foam squares, attach bottom edge of green printed paper grass border to bottom of each layout page as shown. In the same manner, attach remaining grass to layout as shown.

Adhere brown scalloped egg to center of left layout page. Using foam squares, attach floral scalloped egg to brown egg.

Ink edges of pink sitting bunny pink. Ink edges of yellow sitting bunny light brown. Cut ribbon in half; wrap one length around pink bunny's neck; tie in knot and V-notch ends. Adhere pink layer over yellow layer. Using foam squares, attach to left layout page as shown.

Ink edges of pink standing bunny pink. Ink edges of yellow standing bunny light brown. Wrap remaining ribbon around pink bunny's neck; tie in knot and V-notch ends. Adhere pink layer over yellow layer. Using foam squares, attach to right layout page as shown.

Ink edges of each chick light brown. Adhere layers of corresponding bow sizes as desired. Adhere a layered bow to each chick. Using foam squares, attach chicks to layout pages as shown. Add eyes to chicks and bunnies by attaching gems.

Ink edges of top layers of eggs as desired. Adhere top layers of eggs to brown layers. Using foam squares, attach to right layout page as shown. Ink edges of top layers of flowers as desired. Adhere inked flowers to corresponding brown layers. Using foam squares, adhere flowers to top left and right corners of layout as shown. Ink edges of yellow "Happy Easter" light brown; adhere to brown layer. Using foam squares, attach layered title to upper right corner of left layout page. Move grass blades over and under bunnies, chicks and eggs as desired. ●

Source: Cricut machine and cartridge from Provo Craft.

Skill Level
Intermediate

Materials
- Cricut Expression machine
- Cartridges: Destinations (#2000022), Independence Day Seasonal (#2000319), Serenade Solutions (#29-1059)
- Card stock: cream, white, pink, brown, black, light brown
- Printed papers: dark aqua, light aqua, red, dark pink
- Journaling line rubber stamp
- Gray ink pad
- Adhesive foam squares
- Paper adhesive

D.C. Trip

This layout—featuring images of national monuments and cherry blossoms— is the perfect way to showcase treasured photographs of your vacation in our nation's capital.

Design by **Melanie Brown**

Use two 12 x12-inch sheets of cream card stock as layout base. Cut two 11¾ x11½-inch rectangles of light aqua printed paper; adhere as shown to layout base. Cut three 6¼ x 4¼-inch rectangles from white card stock; adhere to red printed paper; trim small borders. Adhere to layout as shown.

Using Independence Day Seasonal cartridge and cream card stock, cut an 11½-inch Capital building. Press "<Capital>." Cut an 11½-inch Capital Building layer from white card stock by pressing "<CptlLyr>."

Using Destinations cartridge and cream card stock, cut a 3-inch "Washington DC" rectangle by pressing "<WshgtnDC>." Cut a rectangle bottom layer in the same manner, using dark aqua printed paper and pressing "<shift>" and "<WshgtnDC>."

Cut a 3-inch "Washington DC" rectangle middle layer from white card stock by selecting Layers feature; press "<WshgtnDC>." Repeat cut using cream card stock.

Cut a 3-inch "Washington DC" rectangle landscape layer from red printed paper by selecting layers feature; press "<shift>" and "<WshgtnDC>." Repeat using black card stock.

Cut a 3-inch "District of Columbia" journaling tag from cream card stock by selecting Country 1 feature; press "<WshgtnDC>."

Cut a 3-inch "District of Columbia" journaling tag layer from red printed paper by selecting Country 1 feature; press "<Shift>" and "<WshgtnDC>."

Using Serenade Solutions cartridge and pink card stock, cut three 3½-inch cherry blossom trees by pressing "<tree3>." Repeat cut using dark pink printed paper. In the same manner, cut one tree from dark pink printed paper at 3-inch setting; cut two trees from dark pink printed paper at 2¾-inch setting and two trees from pink card stock at 2½-inch setting.

Cut top layers of cherry blossom trees using light brown card stock. Repeat all cuts as stated above, pressing "<shift>" and "<tree3>."

Adhere white Capital building to cream layer. Cut layered image in half 5½ inches from bottom right corner. Adhere to layout as shown.

Assemble layers of "Washington DC" rectangle as shown. Using foam squares, attach to upper left corner of layout. Adhere cream layer of "District of Columbia" journaling tag over red layer. Stamp journaling lines onto a 2½ x 2½-inch square of white card stock; adhere journaling tag over stamped square.

Assemble trees, adhering light brown layer over pink layers. Adhere to layout as shown, using foam squares as desired. ●

Source: Cricut machine and cartridges from Provo Craft.

Cinco De Mayo

Capture the memories of your fiesta in a layout created with bright and festive colors!

Design by **Sue Helfrich**

Use a 12 x 12-inch sheet of red card stock for layout base. Cut an 11¾ x 11¾-inch piece of yellow card stock; ink edges; adhere to layout base.

Cut a 7¼ x 5¼-inch rectangle of blue card stock. Cut a 7 x 5-inch rectangle of red card stock. Ink edges of both rectangles; layer red rectangle onto blue rectangle using foam squares. Attach to layout as shown.

Referring to photo, wrap ribbon around bottom of page; secure ends to back of page. In the same manner, wrap red rickrack around page above ribbon.

Using Ashlyn's Alphabet cartridge and red card stock, cut 1½-inch "C, c, e, y" by pressing "<Shift Lock>" and "<c>." Release "<Shift Lock>." Press "<c>," "<e>" and "<y>."

Cut 1½-inch "M, i, o, o" from green card stock; press "<Shift Lock>" and "<m>." Release "<Shift Lock>." Press "<i>," "<o>" and "<o>."

Cut 1½-inch "D, n, a" from blue card stock; press "<Shift Lock>" and "<d>." Release "<Shift Lock>." Press "<n>" and "<a>."

Cut 1½-inch "Cinco De Mayo" shadow from white card stock by selecting Shadow feature. Press "<Shift Lock>," "<c>," "<d>" and "<m>." Release "<Shift Lock>." Press "<i>," "<n>," "<c>," "<o>," "<e>," "<a>," "<y>" and "<o>."

Using Old West cartridge and brown card stock, cut two 8-inch guitars by selecting Icon feature; press "<y>." Cut 8-inch guitar layer from light brown card stock by selecting Icon feature; press "<shift>" and "<y>."

Using Designer Calendar cartridge and blue card stock, cut a 4-inch "5 de Mayo" title. Select Events feature; press "<Monday>." Repeat cut using white card stock.

Cut a 3-inch Mexican hat from red card stock by selecting Events feature. Press "<shift>" and "<Monday>." Repeat with white card stock.

Cut a 2½-inch Mexican hat from blue card stock by selecting Events feature. Press "<shift>" and "<Monday>." Repeat with white card stock.

Adhere colored letters to their shadows. Use Cuttlebug and Swiss Dots embossing folder to emboss letters. Using foam squares, attach letters to top of layout as shown.

Ink edges of guitar and guitar layers. Use watermark pen and marker to make details on guitar layer. Assemble guitar, using foam squares between brown layers; adhere to layout as shown.

Using Cuttlebug and embossing folder, emboss blue "5 de Mayo;" ink edges and adhere offset to white layer. Attach over ribbon and rickrack using foam squares.

Skill Level

Intermediate

Materials

- Cricut Expression machine
- Cartridges:
  Designer Calendar (#29-1055),
  Ashlyn's Alphabet (#29-0831),
  Old West (#29-1549)
- Cuttlebug machine
- Swiss Dots embossing folder (#37-1604)
- Card stock: red, yellow, blue, green, brown, light brown, white
- Brown ink pad
- Black fine-tip marker
- Watermark pen
- 14 inches 1½-inch-wide green/ white dots grosgrain ribbon
- Rickrack: 14 inches ⁷⁄₁₆-inch-wide red, 9½ inches ⅛-inch-wide yellow
- Craft sponge
- Adhesive foam squares
- Paper adhesive

Ink edges of all Mexican hats. Adhere yellow rickrack to each colored hat as shown. Adhere colored hats offset to white layers. Using two layers of foam squares, attach to layout as shown. ●

Sources: Card stock from Core'dinations; Cricut machine and cartridges, Cuttlebug machine and embossing folder from Provo Craft.

Brand New Mama

Capture precious first moments between Mother and Baby with this sweet layout.

Design by **Natalie Malan**

Use a 12 x 12-inch sheet of Happy Birthday Celebrations paper as layout base.

Using Mother's Day Seasonal Cartridge and hot pink floral paper, cut a 7-inch frame by pressing "<Frame3>." Cut a 6-inch flower from white card stock by pressing "<Flower1>." Cut a 2-inch "Mama" title from white card stock by pressing "<Mama>." In the same manner, cut "Mama" layer from hot pink floral paper by pressing "<MamaShadow>."

Using Easter Seasonal cartridge, cut a 3-inch scalloped circle from white card stock. Press "<Circle3>."

Using Sentimentals cartridge and white card stock, cut a 1¼-inch crown. Turn Real Dial size on; select Layers feature; press "<Letter1>."

Adhere scalloped circle to layout as shown.

Cut an 8⅝ x 9½-inch piece of Beautiful Gorgeous paper; tear off one short edge. Adhere to layout as shown, overlapping scalloped circle. Adhere white flower to layout as shown.

Adhere a piece of white card stock to back of hot pink frame. Using teal thread, machine-stitch around frames oval. Adhere frame to layout, overlapping flower.

Using teal thread, machine-stitch through layout along torn edge and one long edge of Beautiful Gorgeous piece with varying lengths of straight and zigzag stitches. Using tan thread, machine-stitch around scalloped circle as shown.

Using tan thread and zigzag stitching, attach 6-inch length of sheer pink fabric to layout as shown. Tie 14-inch length of pink fabric in a bow; V-notch ends. Adhere to layout as shown.

Apply glitter glue to crown. Adhere to center of bow. Adhere white "Mama" layer to pink layer. Adhere over sheer ribbon.

Hand-print, or use a computer to generate, "Brand" and "New" onto white paper; cut rectangles around words. Adhere above "Mama." Adhere buttons as desired. ●

Skill Level
Easy

Materials
- Cricut Expression machine
- Cartridges: Mother's Day Seasonal (#2000101), Sentimentals (#2000067), Easter Seasonal (#2000100)
- White card stock
- White paper
- Printed papers: Quite Contrary Mary Mary Beautiful Gorgeous and Happy Birthday Celebrations, hot pink floral
- Black fine-tip pen
- 7 buttons
- 1½-inch-wide torn silk fabric: 14 inches pink, 6 inches sheer pink
- Thread: teal, tan
- Sewing machine
- Silver glitter glue
- Paper adhesive
- Computer and printer (optional)

Sources: Quite Contrary Mary Mary printed papers from My Mind's Eye; Cricut machine and cartridges from Provo Craft.

Mom's Day Out

Create this sweet and simple layout to showcase a special mom's day out.

Design by **Summer Fullerton**

Use a 12 x 12-inch sheet of green card stock as layout base. Adhere a 7½ x 11-inch piece of printed paper to right half of layout.

Cut two 4 x 6-inch pieces of white card stock; adhere both to light blue card stock and trim small borders. Adhere rectangles to layout as shown; add photos.

Using Doodletype cartridge and navy blue card stock, cut a 1½-inch title "moms" by selecting Book Plate feature; press "<m>," "<o>," "<m>" and "<s>." At the same size, cut "day out" from navy blue card stock by pressing "<d>," "<a>," "<y>," "<o>," "<u>" and "<t>."

Using Plantin SchoolBook cartridge and teal card stock, cut a 2-inch apostrophe by pressing "<shift>" and "<8>." Cut a 3-inch tag from kraft card stock by pressing "<tag1>."

Using Sweet Treats cartridge, cut 2-inch flower from navy blue card stock by pressing "<Flower4>." Repeat cut at 2½-inch setting using light blue card stock and at 3-inch setting using lavender card stock. Cut a 2-inch circle from light yellow card stock by pressing "<shift>" and "<Flower4>." Repeat cut at 2½-inch setting and 3-inch setting. Cut a 2-inch top layer for flower from yellow card stock by selecting Layers feature; press "<Flower4>." Repeat cut at 2½-inch setting and 3-inch setting.

Adhere teal card stock to back of each "moms" bookplate letters; link letters together using white brads. Using foam squares, attach to layout as shown. Adhere apostrophe to "s" letter plate. Adhere "day out" under "mom's" title.

Adhere top two layers of flowers together; decorate with pearls. Using foam squares, attach top layers of flowers to bottom layers. Cut ribbon as follows: 9½ inches, 8½ inches and 7¼ inches. Adhere ribbons to backs of flowers.

Adhere flowers to layout as shown, using foam squares on one. Do not secure centers of ribbons to layout.

Add journaling to tag. String tag onto twine; wrap around ribbons; tie bow. ●

Sources: Card stock from Bazzill Basics Paper Inc. and Jillibean Soup; printed paper and ribbon from Jillibean Soup; Cricut machine and cartridges from Provo Craft.

Skill Level
Easy

Materials
- Cricut Expression machine
- Cartridges:
  Doodletype (#29-0054),
  Sweet Treats (#29-1557),
  Plantin SchoolBook (#29-0390)
- Card stock: lavender, navy blue, light blue, yellow, dark yellow, teal, kraft, green
- Egg Drop Green Onion double-sided printed paper
- 25¼ inches ½-inch-wide green/white polka-dot ribbon
- 12 inches twine
- 4 white brads
- 8 assorted flat-back pearls
- Piercing tool
- Adhesive foam squares
- Paper adhesive

Fabulous

This chic and stylish-looking layout is the ideal
way to highlight Mom's personal flair for fashion.

Design by **Sue Helfrich**

Use a 12 x 12-inch sheet of red card stock as layout base. Cut an 11½ x 11½-inch square of Divine Impressions card stock; adhere to black card stock; trim a small border. Adhere to layout base. Adhere 14-inch length of red ribbon across bottom of layout, securing ends to back. Adhere black/white dots ribbon over red ribbon, securing ends to back.

Using Forever Young cartridge and black card stock, cut a 10-inch mirror. Press "<Mirror>." Cut a 10-inch white mirror layer from flower center using white card stock. Select Layer feature; press "<Mirror>." Cut a 10-inch red mirror shadow from red card stock by selecting Shadow feature; press "<Mirror>."

Skill Level
Intermediate

Materials
- Cricut Expression machine
- Cartridge: Forever Young (#2000065)
- Card stock: black, white, red
- Embossed card stock: Divine Impressions white, Eyelet Impressions red
- Black/white floral printed card stock
- Ribbon: 14 inches 1⁷⁄₁₆-inch-wide red, 6 inches ⅛-inch-wide red, 14 inches ⅜-inch-wide black/white dots
- 6 inches white tulle
- Self-adhesive silver crystals: 3 small, 1 mini
- Adhesive foam squares
- Paper adhesive

Cut a 10-inch flower from Eyelet Impressions card stock by selecting Layer feature; press "<shift>" and "<Mirror>."

Cut a 2-inch "fabulous" from Eyelet Impressions card stock by selecting Word feature; press "<Flower7>." Repeat cut using black card stock.

Cut a 9½-inch model from black card stock by pressing "<Model19>." Cut a 9½-inch model from red card stock by selecting Shadow feature; press "<Model19>." Cut a 9½-inch dress from black/white floral card stock by pressing "<shift>" and "<Model19>." Cut a 9½-inch skirt from black/white floral card stock by selecting Layers feature; press "<Model19>." Repeat cut using white card stock for flower.

Cut a 1½-inch hat from black card stock by selecting Flip feature; press "<Hat2>." Cut a 1½-inch layer for hat from white card stock by selecting Flip feature; press "<shift>" and "<Hat2>."

Cut ½-inch flowers from black card stock by selecting both Flip and Layer features; press "<shift>" and "<Hat2>."

Cut a 1½-inch hat band from black card stock by selecting both Flip and Layer features; press "<Hat2>." Repeat cut using white card stock. Cut a 1½-inch shadow for hat from red card stock by selecting Shadow feature; press "<Hat2>."

Cut a 1¾-inch purse from black card stock by selecting Flip feature; press "<Purse2>." Repeat cut.

Cut a 1¾-inch flower from white card stock by selecting Flip feature; press "<shift>" and "<Purse2>." Cut a 1¾-inch small flower from white card stock by selecting Layers feature; press "<Purse2>." Cut a 1¾-inch mini flower from black card stock by selecting Layers feature; press "<shift>" and "<Purse2>." Repeat cut using white card stock.

Cut a 1½-inch "Vogue" tag from Eyelet Impressions card stock by selecting Tag feature; press "<Dressform>." Cut a 1½-inch "Vogue" tag shadow from black card stock by selecting Tag feature; press "<shift>" and "<Dressform>."

Adhere white layer of mirror to black. Using foam squares, attach layered mirror to red mirror shadow. Adhere to layout on right side of layout as shown.

Adhere red "fabulous" offset to black "fabulous." Using foam squares, attach to left side of layout as shown.

Adhere black model to red model shadow. Adhere black/white floral dress to layered model. Using foam squares, attach black/white floral skirt over dress skirt. Attach small white flower to right shoulder with foam square.

Assemble hat by layering black hat over red shadow. Adhere white hat layer to layered hat. Adhere hat band and black flower over white layer. Adhere black mini flower to small white flower; attach to hat band flower using foam squares. Attach hat to model using foam squares. Attach layered model with foam squares to page as shown.

Assemble purse by adhering white flower layer to a purse. Layer black mini flower to small white flower; attach to white flower on purse using foam squares. Adhere white clasp detail to purse. Attach layered purse to remaining purse using foam squares. Using foam squares, attach layered purse above ribbons on lower right corner of layout.

Adhere red "vogue" tag to black tag. String tulle and thin red ribbon through tag hole; tie knot. Using foam squares, attach tag to top of mirror as shown.

Cut a ⅜-inch circle from white card stock; adhere to Eyelet Impression flower using foam squares. Attach layered flower to "vogue" tag as shown using foam squares.

Attach mini crystal to purse and small crystals to hat, dress and tag. ●

Sources: Embossed card stock from Doodlebug Design Inc.; Cricut machine and cartridge from Provo Craft.

Our Wedding Shower

Lovely patterned paper and pearl embellishments are the perfect accents for this page recounting special pre-wedding events.

Design by **Summer Fullerton**

Use a 12 x 12-inch sheet of Pageantry paper as layout base. Cut a 12 x 8-inch piece of Sonata paper; adhere to top of layout base.

Adhere a 12 x 4-inch piece of Venetian paper to layout as shown; adhere photos as desired.

Using Opposites Attract cartridge and pink card stock, cut a 1¾-inch "our wedding shower" title by selecting Upright feature; press "<o>," "<u>," "<r>," "<w>," "<e>," "<d>," "<d>," "<i>," "<n>," "<g>," "<s>," "<h>," "<o>," "<w>," "<e>" and "<r>."

Using Sweet Treats cartridge and light blue iridescent card stock, cut a 3½-inch cake by pressing "<Cake3>." Repeat to cut frosting layer from white card stock by pressing "<shift>" first. Cut a 3½-inch cake plate from dark pink card stock by selecting Layers feature; press "<Cake3>." Repeat to cut swirl details from teal card stock by pressing "<shift>" first.

Using Winter Woodland cartridge and dark pink card stock, cut a 2-inch bird. Press "<shift>" and "<bird3>." Repeat cut.

Adhere "our wedding shower" title to layout as shown. Attach a pearl brad on either side of title and pink sparkle brad as the dot for "i."

Assemble and adhere layers of cake together as shown. Using foam squares, attach to layout as shown. Attach birds to layout as desired, using foam squares. Adhere rhinestone swirls to layout as show. Accent ends of swirls with pearl brads.

Hand-print, or use computer to generate, journaling on strips of white card stock; adhere to layout as shown. ●

Sources: Card stock from Bazzill Basics Paper Inc.; Cappella papers from BasicGrey; rhinestone swirls from Zva Creative; Cricut machine and cartridges from Provo Craft.

Skill Level
Intermediate

Materials
- Cricut Expression machine
- Cartridges:
  Sweet Treats (#29-1557),
  Winter Woodland (#29-1046),
  Opposites Attract (#29-0227)
- Card stock: pink, dark pink, light blue iridescent, teal, white
- Cappella double-sided printed papers: Sonata, Pageantry, Venetian
- Black fine-tip pen
- Self-adhesive rhinestone swirls
- Brads: 6 pearl, 1 pink sparkle
- Piercing tool
- Adhesive foam squares
- Paper adhesive
- Computer and printer (optional)

Celebrate!

Capture the special moments from your wedding day on pages that you'll treasure for years to come.

Design by **Shirlene Jordan**

Use a 12 x 12-inch piece of blue distressed paper for layout base.

Cut a 10¾ x 7¾-inch rectangle of blue/white floral paper. Cut a 10¾ x 1½-inch strip and a 10¾ x ½-inch strip of green dot paper. Adhere strips to top and bottom of floral rectangle as shown. Round corners of rectangle; adhere centered to layout base.

Using Tie the Knot cartridge and blue/white dot paper, cut 1½-inch "Groom Bride" title. Select Monogram feature and press "<CakeBox>." Repeat cut pressing "<Shift>" and "<CakeBox>." Repeat both cuts using black card stock and Monogram Shadow feature.

Cut a 3-inch "I Do" from white/cream dot paper by selecting Tag feature; press "<I o>." Cut a 3-inch branch from black card stock by pressing "<shift>" and "<LvBrds>." Cut 3-inch Love Birds from white/cream dot paper by pressing "<LvBrds>."

Cut a 2-inch "Celebrate" from blue dot paper by pressing "<Celebrte>." Cut a 2-inch shadow for "Celebrate" from black card stock by selecting Blackout/Shadow feature; press "<shift>" and "<Celebrte>."

Ink edge of "I Do" tag; adhere a 4 x 2-inch piece of black card stock to back of tag. Adhere to layout as shown; attach brad through tag hole.

Adhere "Groom Bride" to black card-stock shadow. Place on bottom of layout, overlapping "I Do" tag.

Adhere branch to top of layout as shown. Ink edges of Love Birds; attach over branch.

Adhere blue dot "Celebrate" to its shadow. Adhere to right side of layout under Love Birds on branch. ●

Source: Cricut machine and cartridge from Provo Craft.

Skill level
Easy

Materials
- Cricut Expression machine
- Cartridge: Tie the Knot (#2000064)
- Black card stock
- Printed papers: blue distressed, blue/white dot, blue/white floral, white/cream dot, green dot, blue dot
- Black ink pad
- Silver glitter brad
- Corner rounder
- Paper adhesive

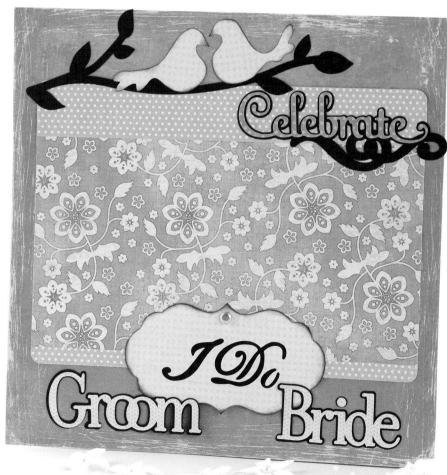

Happily Ever After

A lifetime of love and devotion deserves a special celebration and a memory page to share the legacy with generations to come.

Design by **Miranda Urry**

Use one 12 x 12-inch sheet of black card stock as layout base. Using foam squares, attach an 11½ x 11½-inch square of cream card stock centered to layout base.

Cut an 11 x 11-inch square of black/white polka-dot paper. Wrap both 13-inch lengths of ribbon around polka-dot square as shown; secure ends to back with tape. Using foam squares, attach polka-dot square centered to cream square.

Using Tie the Knot cartridge and floral paper, cut a 10-inch swirl invitation. Select Invitation feature; press "<RSVP>."

Cut a 7½-inch photo card, using light red printed paper, by selecting Card feature; press "<avorBo>." In the same manner, using cream card stock, repeat cut at 7-inch setting. Repeat cut using black card stock at 6½-inch setting.

Cut a 2-inch "Happily" phrase from black card stock by selecting Monogram feature; press "<avorBo>." In the same manner, cut a "Happily" shadow from light red printed paper by selecting Monogram Shadow feature first.

Cut a 2-inch "Ever After" phrase from black card stock by selecting Monogram feature; press "<shift>" and "<avorBo>." In the same manner, cut an "Ever After" shadow from light red printed paper by selecting Monogram Shadow feature first.

Wrap remaining ribbon around swirl invitation; secure ends to back with tape. Using foam squares, attach swirl invitation centered to polka-dot square.

Ink edges of light red picture card black. Using foam squares, attach to layout as shown. In the same manner, attach cream and black picture cards to layout as shown. Adhere photo to black picture card.

Ink edges of light red "Happily" and "Ever After" phrases black. Adhere black phrases over light red shadows. Using foam squares, attach "Happily" to upper left corner of swirl invitation as shown. Attach "Ever After" below layered photo cards using foam squares. Embellish layout with gems. ●

Source: Cricut machine and cartridge from Provo Craft.

Skill Level
Easy

Materials
- Cricut Expression machine
- Cartridge: Tie the Knot (#2000064)
- Card stock: black, cream
- Printed papers: black/white polka-dot, floral, light red
- Black ink pad
- Pink ribbon: 2 (13-inch) lengths ⅛-inch-wide, 1 (10-inch) length ¹⁄₁₆-inch-wide
- 3 decorative gems
- Tape
- Adhesive foam squares
- Paper adhesive

Best Dad

This masculine layout is the perfect way to celebrate any dad!

Design by **Kimber McGray**

Use a 12 x 12-inch sheet of Diced Tomatoes paper as layout base. Cut a 9 x 11-inch rectangle of white card stock; round bottom corners; adhere to base as shown.

Cut a 8⅝ x 10¾-inch rectangle of Peek-a-Boo paper; round bottom corners; adhere to layout as shown. Cut a 3 x 12-inch rectangle of green card stock; sand edges; adhere to layout as shown.

Cut two 5 x 3-inch pieces of white card stock. Adhere photos to white card-stock pieces. Adhere to layout as shown. Cut a 3 x 6¼-inch journaling rectangle from white card stock; adhere to layout as shown.

Using Lyrical Letters cartridge and blue card stock, cut a 3-inch argyle pattern by selecting Capital feature; press "<shift>" and "<Holidays>." Repeat once.

Cut a 2-inch "DAD" from black card stock by selecting Jumbo feature; press "<ShiftLock>," "<D>," "<A>" and "<D>."

Cut a 1½-inch "best" from blue card stock by selecting Italic Monoline feature; press "<b>," "<e>," "<s>" and "<t>."

Using Plantin SchoolBook cartridge and black card stock, cut a ¼-inch circle by pressing "<circle>." Repeat seven times.

Cut a 2-inch tag from black card stock by selecting Roly Poly feature; press "<tagleft>."

Using foam squares, attach argyle patterns to green rectangle. Adhere black circles to centers of argyle diamonds.

Using foam squares, attach "DAD" to layout as shown. Adhere "best" layered over "DAD." Cut tag leaving only 1¼-inch top. Using foam squares, attach tag to journaling rectangle as shown. ●

Sources: Card stock from Core'dinations; printed papers from Jillibean Soup and October Afternoon; Cricut machine and cartridges from Provo Craft.

Skill Level
Easy

Materials
- Cricut Expression machine
- Cartridges:
  Lyrical Letters (#29-0708),
  Plantin SchoolBook (#29-0390)
- Card stock: white, green, blue, black
- Printed papers: Old World Cabbage Stew Diced Tomatoes, Ducks in a Row Peek-a-Boo
- Sandpaper
- Adhesive foam squares
- Paper adhesive

Dad

Colorful, themed layout pages are an ideal way to capture the unique characteristics and personality of your dad.

Design by **Melanie Brown**

Use a 12 x 12-inch sheet of light blue card stock as layout base. Cut an 11½ x 11½-inch square of navy blue card stock; adhere centered to layout base.

Using Life is a Beach cartridge and blue card stock, cut a 3-inch wave by pressing "<shift>" and "<CrusShip>."

Cut a 4-inch sailboat from blue card stock by pressing "<SailBoat>." Cut a 4-inch sailboat layer from cream card stock by selecting Layers feature; press "<SailBoat>." Repeat cut using light blue and red card stock.

Cut a 3-inch anchor from light blue card stock by pressing "<Anchor>." Cut a 3-inch anchor layer from cream card stock by selecting Layer feature; press "<Anchor>."

Cut a 3-inch helm from cream card stock by pressing "<shift>" and "<Anchor>." Cut a 3-inch helm layer from brown card stock by selecting Layers feature; press "<shift>" and "<Anchor>."

Using Old West cartridge, cut an 11½-inch rope frame from cream card stock by selecting Flourish feature; press "<Invited>."

Cut a 3¼-inch "Dad" from cream card stock by selecting Rope feature. Press "<Shift Lock>" and "<d>." Release "<Shift Lock>" and press "<a>" and "<d>."

Ink edges of cream sailboat sails brown; ink edges of light blue sailboat body light blue. Assemble sailboat by adhering following layers to blue sailboat base: cream sails, red flag and light blue body. Adhere layered sailboat to layout as shown.

Adhere wave to bottom edge of navy blue square, overlapping sailboat. Ink edges of both anchor layers brown. Adhere cream layer over light blue layer.

Cut a 6½ x 9-inch piece of multicolored polka-dot paper. Cut a 4¼ x 6¼-inch piece of light blue card stock; adhere to navy blue card stock; trim small border and distress edges. Tie twine around layered rectangle; string layered anchor onto twine; tie in knot. Adhere layered rectangle to multicolored polka-dot rectangle. Adhere to layout as shown.

Ink edges of rope frame brown. Adhere rope frame over multicolored polka-dot rectangle. Adhere brown helm layer over cream helm layer. Ink edges of "Dad" brown. Using foam squares, attach "a" to layered helm. Adhere "Dad" to left edge of layout as shown. ●

Skill Level
Intermediate

Materials
- Cricut Expression machine
- Cartridges:
  Old West (#29-1549),
  Life is a Beach (#29-0707)
- Card stock: navy blue, blue, light blue, brown, cream, red
- Multicolored polka-dot printed paper
- Ink pads: brown, light blue
- 20 inches braided twine
- Distressing tool
- Adhesive foam squares
- Paper adhesive

Source: Cricut machine and cartridges from Provo Craft.

4th of July

The fireworks are hot tonight—sizzling, crackling and bright in the summertime sky!

Design by **Joy Tracey**

Skill Level
Intermediate

Materials
- Cricut Expression machine
- Cartridges:
  Stand and Salute (#29-0961),
  Mini Monograms (#29-0018)
- Card stock: red, white, blue,
  blue printed
- Glitter card stock: light blue,
  cream, red
- Liberty double-sided printed
  papers: Franklin Street,
  Jackson Street
- Annotations stamp set
- Red ink pad
- Pink glitter
- 3 rhinestone stars: medium red,
  medium blue, large blue
- Adhesive foam dots
- Paper adhesive

Use one sheet of 12 x 12-inch blue printed card stock as layout base. Adhere a 12 x 4-inch piece of Franklin Street paper to layout base as shown.

Cut a 3½ x 3½-inch square of white card stock; stamp with journaling lines. Adhere to light blue card stock; trim a small border. Adhere to red card stock; trim a small border. Adhere to layout as shown.

Cut a 5¼ x 7-inch rectangle of Jackson Street paper. Adhere to red card stock; trim a small border. Wrap a 6 x ½-inch strip of Jackson Street paper around bottom of layered rectangle. Secure ends to back. Adhere to layout as shown.

Using Stand and Salute cartridge, cut a 3-inch firecracker border, using cream glitter card stock, by selecting Border feature; press "<shift>" and "<Rocket>."

Cut four 2¼-inch firecracker backgrounds from red card stock by selecting Blackout feature; press "<shift>" and "<Rocket>."

Cut a 4-inch "4th of July" from cream glitter card stock by pressing "<4thofJuly>." In the same manner, cut shadow from red glitter card stock by selecting Shadow feature first.

Cut three 1⅛-inch stars from cream glitter card stock by pressing "<Star>."

Using Mini Monograms cartridge and blue glitter card stock, cut a 5-inch scalloped circle by pressing "<crclsclp>." In the same manner, using white card stock, repeat cut at 5½-inch setting. Repeat cut for final layer using red card stock by selecting Shadow feature first.

Adhere red firecracker layers to back of firecracker border. Detail tops of firecrackers with glitter. Adhere to layout as shown.

Adhere "4th of July" layers and scalloped circle layers together as shown. Adhere to upper left corner of layout. Attach rhinestone stars to cream glitter stars. Adhere to layout as shown. ●

Sources: Card stock from Core'dinations; printed papers from Scenic Route Paper Co.; glitter card stock from Die Cuts With A Veiw; stamp set from Close To My Heart; Cricut machine and cartridges from Provo Craft.

Independence Day

Commemorate the nation's birthday with this layout designed in true patriotic style.

Design by **Sue Helfrich**

Use a 12 x 12-inch sheet of red card stock for layout base. Adhere an 11¾ x 11¾-inch square of blue card stock centered to layout base.

Cut an 11¾ x 1¼-inch strip of embossed card stock. Adhere across bottom of blue square.

Cut blue/white dot ribbon into two lengths, one measuring 6 inches and the other measuring 14 inches. Tie ends of ribbon together; adhere to layout as shown securing ends to back.

Cut a 6 x 4-inch rectangle of embossed card stock; adhere to white card stock; trim a small border. Adhere layered rectangle to dark blue card stock; trim a small border. Adhere to layout as shown. Adhere photo to rectangle.

Using Independence Day cartridge and white card stock, cut six 1¾-inch banner flags. Press "<bannerflag>." Cut six 1¾-inch stripe banner flag layers from embossed card stock by pressing "<stripebannerlyr>." Cut six 1¾-inch star banner flag layers from dark blue card stock by pressing "<starbannerlyr>."

Cut two 10-inch Lady Liberties from dark blue card stock by pressing "<LadyLiberty>." In the same manner, cut a Lady Liberty layer from white card stock by pressing "<LadyLibertylyr>."

Cut a 3½-inch eagle from dark blue card stock by pressing "<Eagle>." In the same manner, and using white card stock, cut an eagle layer by pressing "<EagleLyr>."

Cut two 4¼-inch Liberty Bells from dark blue card stock by pressing "<LibertyBell>." In the same manner, and using white card stock, cut a Liberty Bell layer by pressing "<LibertyBellLry>."

Cut a 2-inch "Independence Day" title from embossed card stock by pressing "<IndpedDay>." Repeat cut using white card stock.

Cut a 4-inch "4th of July" title from embossed card stock by pressing "<4thJuly>." Repeat cut using white card stock.

Tie a knot 1½ inches from each end of red ribbon. Adhere to top of layout as shown. Adhere banner layers as shown. Using foam squares, attach banners over red ribbon.

Ink edges of all remaining white pieces. Adhere white Lady Liberty to a dark blue layer. Adhere remaining dark blue Lady Liberty to left side of layout above embossed strip. Using foam squares, attach layered Lady Liberty as shown.

Ink edges of white eagle layer; adhere over dark blue layer. Using two layers of foam squares, attach to layout as shown.

Ink edges of white Liberty Bell; adhere over a dark blue layer. Using foam squares, attach layered Liberty Bell to remaining dark blue layer. Attach to layout as shown using foam squares.

Ink edges of white "Independence Day" and "4th of July" titles. Adhere white "Independence Day" layer to red layer leaving a small shadow. In the same manner, attach red "4th of July" layer to white layer. Adhere both titles to layout as shown. ●

Source: Cricut machine and cartridge from Provo Craft.

Skill Level
Intermediate

Materials
- Cricut Expression machine
- Cartridge: Independence Day Seasonal (#2000319)
- Card stock: red, white, blue, dark blue
- Red dot embossed card stock
- Brown ink pad
- Ribbon: 20 inches ⅝-inch-wide blue/white dots, 14 inches ⅛-inch-wide red
- Craft sponge
- Adhesive foam squares
- Paper adhesive

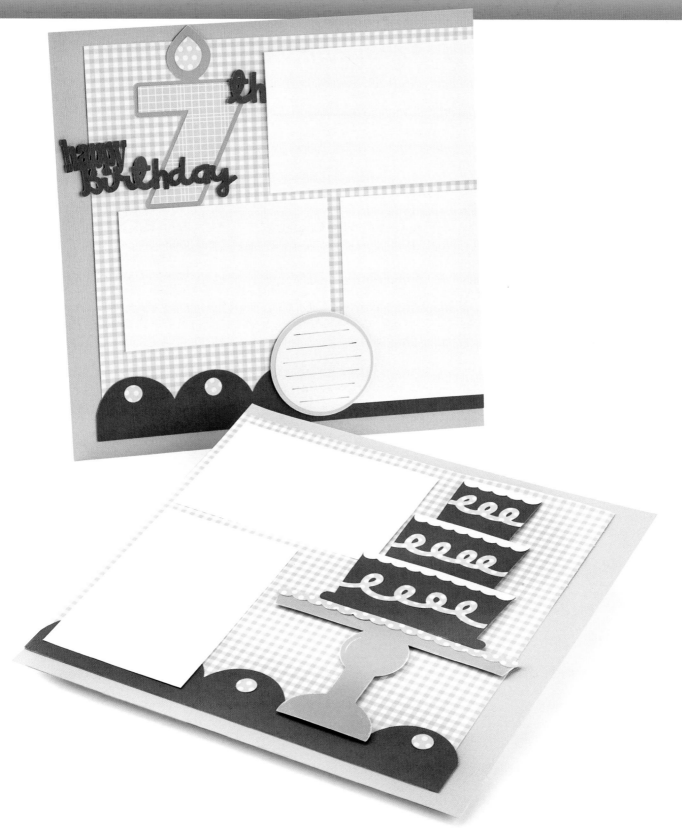

Happy 7th Birthday

No matter how old you are, birthdays are all about the cake!

Design by **Kimber McGray**

Skill Level
Easy

Materials
- Cricut Expression machine
- Cartridges:
  Sweet Treats (#29-1557),
  Plantin SchoolBook (#29-0390)
- Card stock: blue, brown, yellow, gray, white
- Printed papers: Egg Drop Soup Eggs, Soup Staples Light Blue Sugar, Soup Staples Orange Sugar
- Adhesive foam squares
- Paper adhesive

Use two 12 x 12-inch sheets of blue card stock as layout base. Cut two 11 x 11-inch squares of Eggs paper; adhere to layout base as shown.

Using Sweet Treats cartridge and gray card stock, cut a 4-inch cake stand by pressing "<CakePlte>."

Cut a 4-inch scallop for cake stand from Light Blue Sugar paper by selecting Layers feature; press "<CakePlte>."

Cut a 6-inch cake from brown card stock by pressing "<Cake3>."

Cut a 6-inch loopy border for cake from Orange Sugar paper by selecting Layers feature. Press "<shift>" and "<Cake3>." Cut 6-inch scallops for cake from white card stock by pressing "<shift>" and "<Cake3>."

Cut a 5-inch "7" candle from gray card stock by pressing "<7>." In the same manner, cut top layer from Light Blue Sugar paper by pressing "<shift>" first. Cut a 5-inch candle flame from Orange Sugar paper by selecting Layers feature and pressing "<shift>" and "<7>."

Cut a 4-inch "Happy Birthday" from brown card stock by pressing "<HppyBday>." Repeat triming "th" out of one.

Using Plantin SchoolBook cartridge and brown card stock, cut a 1¾-inch scallop border by pressing "<Scallop>." Cut ½-inch circles for border from Orange Sugar paper, by pressing "<Circle>." Repeat four times.

Cut a 3-inch outer circle for journaling from yellow card stock by pressing "<Circle>." Cut a 2¾-inch inner circle for journaling from white card stock by pressing "<Circle>."

Attach ½-inch Orange Sugar circles to brown scalloped edges as show; adhere to lower edge of Eggs paper.

Adhere blue scallop to top of cake stand; using foam squares, attach to right side of layout. Adhere white scallops and yellow loopy border to cake as shown; using foam squares, attach above cake stand.

Adhere layers of "7" candle together. Adhere to upper left corner of layout. Using foam squares, attach intact "Happy Birthday" overlapping lower section of "7" candle. Using foam squares, attach "th" to upper right edge of "7" candle as shown.

Referring to layout, adhere photos as represented by white photo rectangles. Adhere journaling circles together and place overlapping photos and scalloped edge as shown. ●

Sources: Card stock from Core'dinations; printed papers from Jillibean Soup; Cricut machine and cartridges from Provo Craft.

Up for a Swim?

Recall the fun of family vacations at the beach or a day at the pool with friends on these bright and colorful pages!

Design by **Georgina Jarvie**

Skill Level
Intermediate

Materials
- Cricut Expression machine
- Cricut Design Studio
- Cartridges:
  Life is a Beach (#29-0707),
  Tear Drop (#29-0016)
- Card stock: red, bright green, dark green, orange, tan, black, blue pearlescent, silver metallic
- Glitter card stock:
  bright green, yellow
- Printed papers: Double Dot Powder Blue Dot, green dot
- 27 inches ¾-inch-wide red checked ribbon
- 18 inches red string
- Adhesive foam squares
- Paper adhesive

Use two 12 x 12-inch sheets of red card stock as layout base. Adhere a 11¾ x 11¾-inch square of green dot paper to each layout page.

Cut two 11½ x 11½-inch squares of Powder Blue Dot paper. Wrap a 13½-inch length of ribbon horizontally around each square as shown. Secure ends to back and adhere to layout pages.

Cut two 3¾ x 4¾-inch rectangles from bright green card stock. Adhere to green dot paper; trim small borders. Using foam squares, attach layered rectangles to red card stock; trim small borders. Adhere rectangles to right layout page as shown.

Cut a 7¼ x 5¼-inch rectangle of bright green card stock. Adhere to green dot paper; trim a small border. Using foam squares, attach layered rectangle to red card stock; trim a small border. Adhere to left layout page as shown.

Using Tear Drop cartridge, Design Studio and green dot paper, cut a "Up for a Swim?" title. Select Welding feature to nudge letters from "Up for a Swim?" together in following shape properties: Width: 4.244, Height: 2.493, x: .451, y: .375. Cut. Repeat cut using red card stock.

Cut a 3-inch scuba diver using Life is a Beach cartridge and tan card stock by pressing "<ScubaDvr>." Repeat cut using blue pearlescent card stock. Save inside of bubble cuts.

In the same manner, using brown card stock cut hair layer by selecting Layers feature; press "<ScubaDvr>." Repeat cut using bright green card stock, green dot paper and black card stock.

Cut a 2¾-inch fish from red card stock by pressing "<3Fish>." Repeat cut using orange card stock and green glitter card stock. In the same manner, using green glitter card stock cut fish layer by selecting Layers feature; press "<3Fish>." Repeat cut using blue pearlescent card stock and silver metallic card stock.

Cut a 2-inch fish from red card stock by pressing "<2Fish>." Repeat cut using green dot paper.

Cut fish layers at same size setting from blue pearlescent card stock by selecting Layers feature and pressing "<2Fish>." Repeat cut using yellow glitter card stock.

Cut a 2-inch turtle from dark green card stock by pressing "<Turtle>." In the same manner, using bright green card stock cut top layer by selecting Layers feature first.

Cut 1¼-inch turtle charm from bright green card stock by selecting Charm feature; press "<shift>" and "<Turtle>." In the same manner, cut "B", "A" and "Y" charms by selecting Charm feature; press "<ShiftLock>," "<SandDoller>," "<FishBowl>" and "<TikiMask>."

Cut four 1¼-inch charm back layers from Blue Dot paper by selecting Charm feature; press "<shift>" and "<Whale>."

Adhere green dot layer of "Up for a Swim?" title offset to red layer. Adhere above large photo mat on left layout page.

Adhere turtle layers together, adhere to left layout page as shown. Adhere fish layers to fish as desired. Adhere fish to bottom of layout pages, using foam squares as desired. Adhere saved inside bubbles to layout above fish as desired. Adhere layers of scuba diver as shown. Adhere to bottom of right layout page as shown.

Adhere charm backs to charms. Using 3-inch lengths of red string, tie charms to ribbon as shown. Cut remaining string into two lengths; wrap around ribbon on left layout page; tie in knot.

Adhere photos to layout. ●

Sources: Printed papers by Bo-Bunny Press; Cricut machine and cartridges from Provo Craft.

Skill Level
Easy

Materials
- Cricut Expression machine
- Cartridge:
  Cursive 101 (#29-0404)
- Card stock: brown, kraft, red
- Printed papers:
  Minestrone Cannellini beans,
  Alphabet Soup Ground Round,
  Alphabet Soup Vegetable Juice
- Adhesive foam dots
- Paper adhesive

1st Day

A child's first day of school is always filled with anticipation and excitement—a monumental day to be remembered forever.

Design by **Kimber McGray**

Use a 12 x 12-inch sheet of Ground Round paper as layout base.

Using Cursive 101 cartridge and kraft card stock, cut an 11-inch notebook paper background. Select Notebook feature; press "<shift>" and "<library>."

Cut a 3-inch globe from brown card stock by selecting Shadow; press "<shift>" and "<Socialstds>." Cut a 2-inch "1 ay" section of title from red card stock by pressing "<1>," "<a>" and "<y>." Cut a "D" in the same manner, pressing "<shift>" first. Cut a 1-inch "st" and date from red card stock by pressing "<s>," "<t>," "<2>," "<0>," "<1>" and "<0>."

Referring to photo, adhere strips of printed papers and red card stock to back of notebook paper background. Adhere to layout as shown.

Using foam dots, attach "Day" to left edge of notebook background. Adhere "1st" to globe. Using foam dots, attach layered globe to layout next to "Day." Adhere "2010" as shown. Adhere photos to layout as represented by white photo rectangles. ●

Sources: Card stock from Core'dinations and Jillibean Soup; printed papers from Jillibean Soup; Cricut machine and cartridge from Provo Craft.

Learn

Celebrate your child's love of learning with this fun and bright layout!

Design by **Lynn Ghahary**

Use one 12 x 12-inch sheet of blue card stock as layout base.

Using Plantin SchoolBook cartridge, cut two 2 x 2-inch squares from striped paper by pressing "<shift>" and "<square>." Repeat with all printed papers.

Cut a 2-inch flower from yellow card stock by pressing "<flower>." Cut a 2-inch leaf from green card stock by pressing "<shift>" and "<leaf>." Cut a 2-inch apple from red card stock by pressing "<apple>."

Using Graphically Speaking cartridge, cut a 4-inch "Learn" from red card stock by selecting Jumbled feature. Press "<Image09>."

Referring to image, adhere all 2 x 2-inch squares to page. Using foam dots, attach apple, leaf and flower between squares.

Thread white string through button; tie bow and trim ends. Adhere button to flower center. Wrap white string around "L" in "Learn"; tie bow and trim ends. Adhere "Learn" to page as shown. Adhere photos to page as represented by white photo rectangles and squares. ●

Source: Cricut machine and cartridges from Provo Craft.

Skill Level
Easy

Materials
- Cricut Expression machine
- Cartridges:
  Plantin SchoolBook (#29-0390),
  Graphically Speaking (#29-0590)
- Card stock: red, yellow, green, blue, white
- Printed papers: striped, flower, argyle, polka-dot
- Yellow button
- White string
- Adhesive foam dots
- Paper adhesive

Bon Voyage

Set sail down memory lane with layout pages that commemorate your vacation of a lifetime.

Design by **Georgina Jarvie**

Use two 12 x 12-inch sheets of brown printed paper as layout base. Cut two 11¾ x 11¾-inch squares of light blue card stock; adhere centered to each layout base.

Cut a 7 x 5-inch rectangle of brown/blue printed paper. Adhere to yellow card stock; trim a small border; ink edges. Adhere to brown printed paper; trim a small border. Adhere to left page of layout as shown.

Cut two 4 x 4-inch squares of brown/blue printed paper. Adhere squares to yellow card stock; trim small borders; ink edges. Adhere squares to brown printed paper; trim small borders. Adhere squares to right page of layout as shown.

Using Don Juan cartridge, cut a 1½-inch "Bon Vyage!" using yellow card stock. Press "<B>," "<o>," "<n>," "<v>," "<y>," "<a>," "<G>," "<e>" "<shift>" and "<1>." Cut shadow in the same manner, using navy blue card stock and selecting Shadow feature first.

Using Life Is a Beach cartridge and yellow card stock, cut a 1½-inch helm. Press "<shift>" and "<Anchor>." Cut a helm layer in the same manner, using brown card stock and selecting Layers feature first.

Cut a 4½-inch cruise ship from cream card stock by pressing "<CrusShip>." In the same manner, cut a cruise ship base from black card stock by selecting Layers feature first.

Cut two 3-inch waves from navy blue card stock. In Settings, change mat size to 12 x 24. Press "<shift>" and "<CrusShip>."

Cut a 4-inch set of seagulls from cream card stock by pressing "<shift>" and "<LightHse>."

Cut a 1½-inch pelican from yellow card stock by selecting Flip feature; press "<Pelican>." In the same manner, from cream card stock cut a pelican layer, selecting Layers feature first. Repeat layer cut using black card stock.

Skill level
Easy

Materials
- Cricut Expression machine
- Cartridges:
  Life is a Beach (#29-0707),
  Don Juan (#29-0425)
- Card stock: yellow, light blue,
  navy blue, cream, black, brown,
  light brown, gray
- Printed papers: brown,
  brown/blue
- Brown ink pad
- Craft sponge
- Adhesive foam squares
- Paper adhesive

Cut a 2½-inch roosting stump from brown card stock by pressing "<shift>" and "<Pelican>." In the same manner, using light brown card stock cut a layer for stump by selecting Layer feature first.

Ink edges of "Bon Vyage!"; adhere to navy blue shadow.

Adhere helm layers together as shown. Using helm as "O" in "Voyage," adhere "Voyage" to top of right layout page as shown. Adhere "Bon" to top of left layout page as shown.

Ink cream cruise ship edges. Cut a 6 x 1-inch piece of gray card stock; adhere to back of black cruise ship, covering holes. Assemble cruise ship layers as shown. Adhere 1⅝ inches from left side of bottom left layout page.

Ink edges of tan stump layer; adhere to stump. Adhere stump to layout as shown.

Ink edges of yellow and cream pelican layers. Assemble pelican as shown. Using foam squares, attach above stump.

Trim waves to 11¾-inch lengths. Using foam squares, attach to bottom of each layout page.

Ink edges of seagulls. Using foam squares, adhere to layout as shown. Adhere photos to layout. ●

Source: Cricut machine and cartridges from Provo Craft.

Autumn Splendor

Whimsical autumn motifs frame photographs of outdoor fun when the leaves are turning beautiful shades of orange, red and yellow.

Design by **Melanie Brown**

Skill Level
Intermediate

Materials
- Cricut Expression machine
- Cartridges:
  Give a Hoot (#2000098),
  Songbird (#2000063)
- Card stock: lavender, dark brown
- Polka-dot printed papers: purple, lavender, red, orange, yellow, brown, dark brown, light brown, black
- Inks pads: brown, orange, purple
- Black fine-tip marker
- 2 (10-inch) lengths 1¼-inch-wide white and orange striped ribbon
- Adhesive foam squares
- Paper adhesive

Use a 12 x12-inch sheet of dark brown card stock as layout base.

Cut a 11½ x 11½-inch square of yellow polka-dot paper; adhere centered to layout base.

Cut two 6¼ x 4¼-inch rectangles of brown polka-dot paper; adhere to purple polka-dot paper; trim small borders. Tie a knot 3 inches from one end of each ribbon. Wrap a ribbon around each rectangle; secure ends to back. Adhere rectangles to layout base as shown.

Using Give a Hoot cartridge and dark brown polka-dot paper, cut a 6¾-inch tree base by pressing "<tree4>." Cut a 6¾-inch tree top layer from red polka-dot paper by pressing "<shift>" and "<tree4>." Cut a 6¾-inch tree layer from orange paper by selecting Layer feature; press "<tree4>." Set leaves aside.

Cut a 2-inch raccoon from lavender polka-dot paper by pressing "<Raccoon1>." Cut a 2-inch set of raccoon layers from purple polka-dot paper by pressing "<shift>" and "<Raccoon1>." Cut a 2-inch second set of raccoon layers from lavender card stock by selecting Layer feature; press "<shift>" and "<Raccoon1>." Cut 2-inch raccoon eyes and nose from black card stock by selecting Layer feature; press "<Raccoon1>."

Cut a 1¾-inch tree stump from dark brown polka-dot paper by selecting Accent feature; press "<Bear>." Cut a 1¾-inch top layer of stump from brown polka-dot paper by selecting Accent feature; press "<shift>" and "<Bear>."

Cut a 1¾-inch squirrel from dark brown polka-dot paper by pressing "<Sqrrell1>." Cut a 1¾-inch squirrel layer from dark brown card stock by pressing "<shift>" and "<Sqrrell1>." Cut a 1¾-inch second squirrel layer from light brown polka-dot paper by selecting Layer feature; press "<Sqrrell1>." Cut a 1¾-inch last squirrel layer from brown polka-dot paper by selecting Layer feature; press "<shift>" and "<Sqrrell1>."

Cut a 3-inch acorn from light brown polka-dot paper by selecting Accent feature; press "<Sqrrell1>." Cut a 3-inch acorn top from dark brown polka-dot paper by selecting Accent feature; press "<shift>" and "<Sqrrell1>."

Using Songbird cartridge and orange polka-dot paper, cut a 1¼-inch "Splendor." Press "<Shift Lock>" and "<s>." Release "<Shift Lock>" and press "<p>," "<l>," "<e>," "<n>," "<d>," "<o>" and "<r>." In the same manner, cut shadow for "Splendor" from brown polka-dot paper by selecting Shadow feature.

Cut a 1¼-inch "Autumn" from red polka-dot paper by pressing "<Shift Lock>" and "<a>." Release "<Shift Lock>" and press "<u>," "<t>," "<u>," "<m>" and "<n>." In the same manner, cut shadow for "autumn" from brown polka-dot paper by selecting Shadow feature.

Assemble tree as shown; ink edges orange. Using foam squares, attach with base of tree to layout base 2½ inches from lower right side.

Adhere raccoon layers to lavender polka-dot raccoon base. Adhere to lower right corner of layout, next to tree. Adhere brown stump layer to top of dark brown stump. Adhere to lower left corner of layout as shown.

Assemble squirrel layers as shown; add an eye using black marker. Ink edges brown. Using foam squares, attach squirrel atop stump. Adhere dark brown acorn top to light brown acorn. Attach using foam squares as shown.

Adhere "Autumn Splendor" letters to their shadows. Adhere "Autumn Splendor" as shown, layering letters so they appear to flow together. Add cut-out leaves to bottom of layout as shown. ●

Source: Cricut machine and cartridges from Provo Craft.

Paris

Whether you're traveling close to home or around the world, create treasured keepsake layouts to capture all your special vacation memories.

Design by **Shirlene Jordan**

Use a 12 x 12-inch sheet of floral paper for layout base. Cut an 11¼ x 11¼-inch piece of gray/white printed paper; adhere to center of layout base.

Cut a 4½ x 7-inch rectangle of dark teal printed paper. Cut a 4⅛ x 5½-inch rectangle of light teal printed paper. Adhere rectangles together as shown. Referring to photo, adhere to lower right corner of layout.

Using Destinations cartridge and gray printed paper, cut a 10-inch Paris image by pressing "<Paris>."

Cut a 10-inch landscape layer from green printed paper by selecting Layers feature; press "<shift>" and "<Paris>." Cut a 10-inch sun and rectangle layer from yellow printed paper by selecting Layers feature; press "<Paris>."

Cut a 7½-inch Eiffel Tower from metallic silver card stock by selecting Sites feature; press "<Paris>." Cut a 2¼-inch France circle from yellow printed paper by selecting Country 1 feature; press "<Paris>." Cut a 2¼-inch luggage tag from striped paper by selecting Location feature; press "<shift>" and "<Paris>."

Using Forever Young cartridge and silver metallic card stock, cut a 2-inch "ooh la la." Select Word feature and press "<Hat1>." Cut a 2-inch shadow "ooh la la" from green printed paper by selecting Word feature; press "<shift>" and "<Hat1>."

Skill Level
Easy

Materials
- Cricut Expression machine
- Cartridges: Destinations (#2000022), Forever Young (#2000065)
- Silver metallic card stock
- Printed papers: gray, white/ gray, green, yellow, light teal, dark teal, multicolored striped, multicolored floral
- Brown string
- Adhesive foam squares
- Paper adhesive

Assemble Paris rectangle. Cut a 5¼ x 7¼-inch rectangle of light teal printed paper. Adhere yellow sun to upper left corner of light teal rectangle. Adhere green landscape layer to bottom edge of light teal rectangle. Adhere yellow rectangle to reverse side of "Paris" section of gray Paris image. Adhere gray Paris image to layered teal rectangle as shown. Referring to photo, adhere layered Paris image to layout.

Using foam squares, attach silver metallic Eiffel Tower to Paris image. Layer silver metallic "ooh la la" to its green shadow. Adhere above layered teal rectangles.

Assemble luggage tag so it hooks through France circle. Wrap brown string through luggage tag loop; tie in knot. Adhere tagged France loop to layout overlapping lower right corner of teal rectangle. ●

Source: Cricut machine and cartridges from Provo Craft.

Family Time

Create quick and easy pages to capture your most special family moments.

Design by **Keri Lee Sereika**

Use a 12 x 12-inch sheet of light green card stock as layout base.

Cut a 12 x 6¾-inch piece of printed paper. Cut a 12 x 1½-inch strip of dark brown card stock, punch one long edge with Treading Water Border punch. Adhere to underside of printed paper.

Wrap 24 inches of brown ribbon around top of printed paper and secure ends to back; adhere to layout base as shown. Create faux bow by folding ends of a 6½-inch piece of ribbon into middle. Wrap a 1-inch length of ribbon around center; attach using adhesive dot; adhere to layout.

Adhere a 12 x ¾-inch piece of dark brown card stock to layout 1⅜ inches from top edge.

Cut an 8 x 2-inch rectangle of kraft card stock; using Admission for One punch, punch corners. Sponge ink along edges. Pierce three holes at each end of kraft rectangle; insert brads.

Cut 2½-inch "Family Time" using A Child's Year cartridge and dark teal card stock. Select Font feature and press "<StckHrse>." Adhere to kraft rectangle; attach to center top of layout using foam squares. Adhere buttons to bottom left of layout. Adhere photos to page as represented by dark teal photo rectangles. ●

Sources: Printed paper from October Afternoon; chalk ink pad from Clearsnap Inc.; punches from Fiskars; Cricut machine and cartridge from Provo Craft.

Skill Level
Easy

Materials
- Cricut Expression machine
- Cartridge: A Child's Year (#29-0833)
- Card stock: kraft, dark brown, light green, dark teal
- Farm Fresh South Forty double-sided printed paper
- Olive green chalk ink pad
- Black fine-tip marker
- 6 brown brads
- 3 light blue buttons
- 31½ inches ⅝-inch-wide brown satin ribbon
- Punches: Treading Water Border, Admission for One
- Piercing tool
- Craft sponge
- Adhesive foam squares
- Adhesive dots
- Paper adhesive

Touch Down

What goes better with fall than football?

Design by **Shirlene Jordan**

Use a 12 x 12-inch sheet of orange printed paper as layout base. Round corners of an 11 x 11-inch piece of green printed paper; adhere to layout.

Cut a 10¾ x 1½-inch piece and a 9½ x 1½-inch strip of multicolored stripe paper. Adhere to layout as shown.

Using Sports Mania cartridge and orange/white printed paper, cut a 6-inch "Hooray!" photo square by selecting Background feature; press "<Flag>."

Cut a 4-inch "TOUCH DOWN!" title from tan/brown grid paper by pressing "<shift>" and "<Football>." To cut title shadow, repeat cut from dark brown card stock by selecting Shadow feature; press "<shift>" first. In the same manner, cut goal post from white card stock by selecting Layer feature; press "<shift>" and "<Touchdown>."

Cut a 3-inch football from dark brown card stock by selecting Shadow feature; press "<Football>." In the same manner, cut football layer from white card stock by selecting Blackout feature; press "<Football>." Using tan/brown grid paper, cut 3-inch football by pressing "<Football>." Repeat cut, using brown printed paper, by selecting Layers feature first.

Cut a 5-inch clipboard from dark brown printed paper by pressing "<shift>" and "<SoccCrnr>." Repeat cut using silver metallic paper. Cut 5-inch notebook paper from cream lined paper by selecting Layers feature; press "<shift>" and "<SoccCrnr>."

Using Designer's Calendar cartridge, cut two 2½-inch leaves from yellow printed paper by pressing "<shift>" and "<September>." Repeat cut using red dot paper at 2¼-inch setting. Repeat cut using light green printed paper at 2-inch setting.

Adhere "Hooray!" photo square to dark brown card stock; trim a small border. Adhere to layout as shown. Cut silver metallic clipboard down to clip section; adhere to dark brown clipboard. Adhere lined paper to clipboard as shown. Adhere clipboard to layout as shown.

Assemble and adhere "TOUCH DOWN!" title layers and goal post as shown. Adhere title to top of layout, overlapping photo square.

Adhere leaves to layout as shown. Assemble and adhere Football layers as shown. Adhere to lower left corner of layout. ●

Sources: Corner rounder from Fiskars; Cricut machine and cartridges from Provo Craft.

Skill Level
Easy

Materials
- Cricut Expression machine
- Cartridges:
  Sports Mania (#29-0521),
  Designers Calendar (#29-1055)
- Cricut Paper Trimmer
- Card stock: dark brown, white
- Silver metallic paper
- Printed papers: orange, red dot, green, light green, yellow, orange/white, multicolored stripe, brown, dark brown, cream lined, tan/brown grid
- Corner rounder
- Paper adhesive

A u t u m n

Celebrate the change of seasons with a page designed around the colors and motifs of autumn.

Design by **Lynn Ghahary**

Skill Level
Easy

Materials
- Cricut Expression machine
- Cartridge: Stretch Your Imagination (#29-0422)
- Card stock: kraft, cream, red, dark brown, rust, light orange
- Printed papers: wood grain, brown/white dot, multicolored striped
- Black fine-tip marker
- Adhesive foam dots
- Paper adhesive

Use one 12 x 12-inch sheet of kraft card stock for layout base.

Adhere a 5½ x 12-inch rectangle of brown/white dot paper to layout base 3½ inches from left edge. Adhere a 1 x 12-inch piece of multicolored striped paper to brown/white dot rectangle ¼ inch from left edge as shown. Adhere photos to layout as represented by white photo rectangles.

Using Stretch Your Imagination cartridge and cream card stock, cut a 5-inch "Autumn" shadow. Select Shadow feature; press "<shift>" and "<Autumn>." Cut a 5-inch "Autumn" from rust card stock by pressing "<shift>" and "<Autumn>."

Cut 5½-inch leaves and acorns from light orange card stock by selecting Layers feature; press "<shift>" and "<Autumn>." Repeat cut with red and dark brown card stock.

Cut a 5-inch tree from wood grain paper by pressing "<Tree>."

Cut 5½-inch leaf layers from light orange card stock by selecting Layers feature; press "<Tree>." Repeat cut using red and rust card stock.

Adhere "Autumn" title to its shadow. Using foam dots, attach a red and a light orange leaf. Adhere brown acorn to end of title. Attach to layout using foam dots. Adhere tree to lower right area of page. Adhere leaves to tree, using foam dots on some leaves. ●

Source: Cricut machine and cartridge from Provo Craft.

Boo 2 You

Display photos of your little goblins in the height of all their Halloween fun with this easy-to-create layout.

Design by **Natalie Malan**

Use a 12 x 12-inch sheet of black flocked damask paper as left layout page base. Use a 12 x 12-inch sheet of green dot paper as right layout page base.

- -

Adhere a 5½ x 12-inch piece of black flocked damask paper to right layout page as shown. Adhere a 4½ x 12-inch piece of orange dot paper over black flocked damask paper on right layout page.

- -

Using Accent Essentials cartridge and green dot paper, cut a 10-inch scalloped frame by pressing "<Accnt47>." Cut a 6-inch crest from black/white diamond paper by pressing "<shift>" and "<Accnt48>."

Cut a 2-inch accent circle from black mini-dot paper by pressing "<shift>" and "<Accnt6>." Repeat cut at 3-inch setting. Cut a 5-inch slanted layered square from black mini-dot paper by pressing "<Accnt44>." Repeat cut using black/white diamond paper.

Using Storybook cartridge and green dot paper, cut a 2-inch "2" by pressing "<2>."

Skill Level
Intermediate

Materials
- Cricut Expression machine
- Cartridges:
  Gypsy Font Digital (#29-1080),
  Sentimentals (#2000067),
  Storybook (#29-0589),
  Black Letter (#29-0711),
  Winter Woodland (#29-1046),
  Accent Essentials (#29-0391)
- Card stock: black, white
- Printed papers: orange dot, black flocked damask, green dot, black mini-dot, black/white diamond
- 2 green paper flowers
- White button
- Ribbon: 23 inches ⅜-inch-wide black/white stitched, 12 inches ⅜-inch-wide green/white stitched, 24 inches ⅝-inch-wide black
- Paper adhesive

Using Gypsy Font Digital cartridge and black card stock, cut a 1½-inch "B" by selecting Monogram feature; press "<b>."

Cut a 2-inch "O" from black card stock by selecting Monogram feature; press "<o>." Repeat cut at 1½-inch setting.

Using Winter Woodland cartridge and black card stock, cut two 1-inch "o"s by selecting Font feature; press "<skater>."

Using Sentimentals cartridge and black card stock, cut a 2¼-inch decorative swirl by selecting Layers feature; press "<Folder>." Repeat cut selecting Flip feature first.

Using Blackletter cartridge and black card stock, cut a 2¾-inch "Y" by pressing "<shift>" and "<y>." Cut a 1½-inch "u" from black card stock by pressing "<u>."

Adhere scalloped frame to layout as shown. Cut a 12 x 7¾-inch piece of orange dot paper; tear off one long edge. Adhere to left layout page over scalloped frame.

Adhere a 7 x 5⅛-inch piece of white card stock to crest; this will be a photo mat. Adhere layered crest to layout as shown. Adhere decorative swirls over layered crest. Adhere a paper flower to 2-inch accent circle. Adhere over decorative swirls as shown.

Tie a bow with a 5½-inch length of black/white stitched ribbon. Adhere bow to decorative swirl.

Adhere 2-inch "O" to 3-inch accent circle. Adhere "2" over layered accent circle. Adhere to left layout page as shown. Adhere "Boo" to layout above layered "2" accent circle.

Adhere four pieces of slanted layered squares to right layout page as shown, saving a center square. Adhere 12-inch length of green/white stitched ribbon and black ribbon to right layout page as shown.

Cut two 6 x 4-inch rectangles from white card stock to be used as photo mats. Adhere photo mats to right layout page, overlapping slanted squares and ribbons.

Adhere remaining paper flower to right layout page as shown. Adhere remaining black ribbon to left layout page as shown. Adhere a 12-inch length of black/white stitched ribbon over black ribbon. Adhere saved slanted square center to back of white button. Tie a bow with remaining black/white stitched ribbon; adhere to button. Attach layered button to left layout page as shown. ●

Source: Cricut machine and cartridges from Provo Craft.

Best Birthday Ever

Forever capture your "Happy Birthday" moments!

Design by **Sue Helfrich**

Use a 12 x 12-inch sheet of brown card stock as layout base. Adhere an 11¾ x 11¾-inch square of rust floral paper centered to layout base. Wrap a 16-inch length of 1⁷⁄₁₆-inch-wide brown satin ribbon around left edge of layout; adhere ends to back. Using remaining 20-inch length of 1⁷⁄₁₆-inch-wide brown satin ribbon, tie a bow around 16-inch ribbon as shown.

Cut a 7½ x 5½-inch rectangle of cream card stock. Using Cuttlebug embossing machine and Swiss Dots embossing folder, emboss cream rectangle; ink edges brown. Adhere to rust card stock; trim a small border. Using foam squares, attach layered rectangle to an 8½ x 6-inch piece of brown card stock. Adhere to layout as shown.

Using Stamping Solutions cartridge and brown card stock, cut a 3½-inch "Happy Birthday" by pressing "<HpyBday>." In the same manner, repeat cut using cream card stock, selecting Shadow feature first.

Using Lyrical Letters cartridge and cream card stock, cut a 3-inch "best" by selecting Jumbo feature; press "<Thanks>." Repeat cut using brown card stock.

Using Tie the Knot cartridge and cream card stock, cut a 2½-inch "Ever" by selecting Monogram feature; press "<shift>" and "<avorBo>." Repeat cut using brown card stock, selecting Monogram Shadow feature first.

Cut a 2¼-inch blossom from cream card stock by pressing "<Blossom1>." In the same manner, cut blossom top layer by pressing "<shift>" first. Repeat cuts at 2½-inch setting.

Cut a 1½-inch tag from cream card stock by selecting Tag feature and pressing "<Heart1>."

Cut a 1½-inch tag shadow from rust card stock by selecting Tag feature and pressing "<avorbo>."

Ink edges of all cream pieces brown.

Trim "Birthday" from both Happy Birthday cuts. Using foam squares, attach brown "Birthday" to cream shadow. Using two layers of foam squares, attach "Birthday" to layout as shown.

Trim "best" from both cuts. Adhere cream "best" to brown offset. Using foam squares, attach to layout above "Birthday." Adhere cream "Ever" to brown shadow. Using two layers of foam squares, attach to layout as shown.

Adhere brown blossom layers over cream layers. Using foam squares, attach to top right and bottom corner of layout. Adhere cream tag over rust shadow. Attach to layout as shown, using foam squares. Tie tag to bow with ⅛-inch-wide brown satin ribbon; tie lace around knot. Adhere pearls to layout as shown. ●

Skill Level
Intermediate

Materials
- Cricut Expression machine
- Cartridges:
  Tie the Knot (#2000064),
  Lyrical Letters (#29-0708),
  Sentimentals (#2000067),
  Stamping Solutions (#29-0832)
- Cuttlebug machine
- Embossing folder:
  Swiss Dots (#37-1604)
- Card stock: cream, brown, rust
- Rust floral printed paper
- Brown ink pad
- Ribbon: 36 inches 1⁷⁄₁₆-inch-wide brown satin, 8 inches ⅛-inch-wide brown satin, 8 inches 1¼-inch-wide brown lace
- 7 self-adhesive white pearls
- Craft sponge
- Adhesive foam squares
- Paper adhesive

Source: Cricut machine and cartridges, Cuttlebug machine and embossing folder from Provo Craft.

Harvest Time

Celebrate autumn with a page to commemorate a visit to the apple orchard or a favorite fall festival.

Design by **Keri Lee Sereika**

Project note: When selecting fonts on cartridges with only images on overlay keypad, refer to cartridge handbook to find font key placements.

Use one 12 x 12-inch sheet of dark gold card stock as layout base. Cut an 11½ x 11½-inch piece of light gold card stock; adhere to layout base. Pierce holes to attach brads to each corner of light gold card stock.

Trace round edge of a dinner plate onto one short edge of an 8½ x 6½-inch piece of Root Cellar paper. Using pinking shears, cut edges and semicircle; adhere to layout as shown.

Cut a 1½ x 10⅜-inch strip of Farm House paper. Adhere over left edge of Root Cellar paper on layout. Adhere a 4 x 6-inch piece of dark red card stock to light brown card stock; trim a small border. Adhere photo to red rectangle. Tie ribbon around top of photo; tie bow; V-notch ends. Adhere photo to layout using foam squares.

Using Winter Wonderland cartridge and dark brown card stock, cut 1½-inch "Harvest Time." Select Font Shadow feature and press "<Shift Lock>," "<h>" and "<t>." Release "<Shift Lock>." Press "<a>," "<r>," "<v>," "<e>," "<s>," "<t>," "<i>," "<m>" and "<e>."

Using From My Kitchen cartridge and dark red card stock, cut a 2-inch Apple. Select Shadow/Blackout feature; press "<shift>" and "<Fruit>." Cut 2-inch Apple Center from cream card stock. Select Layers feature; press "<shift>" and "<Fruit>."

Cut a 3¼-inch Apple Journal Spot from dark red card stock. Select Shadow/Blackout feature; press "<shift>" and "<Fruit>." Cut 3¼-inch Apple Center from cream card stock. Select Layers feature; press "<shift>" and "<Fruit>." Stamp journaling lines with chalk ink. Adhere to dark red apple.

Adhere "Harvest Time" title along curve of Root Cellar paper, leaving 2 inches between words.

Color apple stems, seeds and leaves using pearlescent ink. Adhere apple centers to apple bodies.

Write desired text onto Journal Spot Apple with marker. Using foam squares, attach Journal Spot Apple to upper right corner of layout as shown. Using foam squares, attach remaining apple in space left between words. Tie dark green thread through buttons; adhere to bottom right of layout. ●

Skill Level
Easy

Materials
- Cricut Expression machine
- Cartridges: Winter Woodland (#29-1046), From My Kitchen (#29-1054)
- Card stock: light gold, dark gold, tan, dark brown, dark red, cream
- Farm Fresh double-sided printed papers: Root Cellar, Farm House
- Journaling Circles Small Stamp Set
- Brown chalk ink pad
- Pearlescent ink pads: brown, green
- Black fine-tip marker
- 4 black brads
- Buttons: 2 green, 1 red
- 18 inches ½-inch-wide green grosgrain ribbon
- Dark green thread
- Piercing tool
- Pinking shears
- Craft sponge
- Adhesive foam squares
- Paper adhesive

Sources: Printed papers from October Afternoon; stamp set from Hampton Art; ink pads from Clearsnap Inc.; Cricut machine and cartridges from Provo Craft.

Giving Thanks

Create a memory page designed in warm and subtle autumn colors to share photos and thoughts of what you are most thankful for.

Design by **Kimber McGray**

Skill Level
Easy

Materials
- Cricut Expression machine
- Cartridges:
  Cursive 101 (#29-0404),
  Printing Press (#29-0226),
  Doodlecharms (#29-0021)
- Card stock: light brown, dark brown, kraft
- Printed papers: Old World Cabbage Stew Red Peppers double-sided, Lil' Buddy yellow
- Brown ink pad
- Black fine-tip marker
- Twine
- Sandpaper
- Paper adhesive

Use a 12 x 12-inch sheet of light brown card stock as layout base; sand edges. Cut a 10 x 11-inch piece of Red Peppers paper, round bottom corners; adhere to layout base aligning top edges.

Cut a 1¾-inch "G" using Cursive 101 cartridge and dark brown card stock, by pressing "<shift>"and "<g>." To cut 1¾-inch "iving," press "<i>," "<v>," "<i>," "<n>" and "<g>."

Using Printing Press cartridge and Lil' Buddy paper, cut a 1¾-inch "T" by selecting Character feature, press "<shift>" and "<t>." To cut 1¾-inch "hanks," press "<h>," "<a>," "<n>," "<k>" and "<s>."

Cut three 1½-inch oak leaves using Doodlecharms cartridge and light brown card stock, by pressing "<shift>" and "<acornlf>." Repeat with kraft card stock and Red Peppers paper. Ink and sand edges of leaves.

Cut three 1½-inch acorns and leaves; reload light brown card stock into cutter and press "<shift>" and "<acornlf>." Repeat with kraft card stock and Red Peppers paper. Ink and sand edges of acorns and leaves.

Cut a 4-inch oak leaf for journaling; reload piece of kraft card stock into cutter and press "<acornlf>." Wrap twine around stem.

Adhere words, leaves and acorns as shown to layout base. Adhere photos to layout as represented by white photo rectangles. ●

Sources: Card stock from Core'dinations; printed papers from Jillibean Soup and Pebbles Inc.; Cricut machine and cartridges from Provo Craft.

Hanukkah

Cherish your holiday memories amidst these traditional Hanukkah colors and symbols.

Design by **Miranda Urry**

Use a 12 x 12-inch sheet of silver card stock as layout base. Cut an 11½ x 11½-inch square of navy card stock; adhere centered to layout base. Cut an 11 x 11-inch square of silver printed paper; adhere centered to layout.

Using Wild Card cartridge and navy card stock, cut a 7-inch menorah card by pressing "<Hanukkah>."

Cut an 8-inch "Hanukkah" from silver card stock by selecting Phrase feature; press "<shift>" and "<Hanukkah>." Repeat using white card stock at 6-inch setting.

Cut a 6-inch Star of David from navy blue card stock by selecting Icon feature; press "<Hanukkah>." In the same manner, cut two stars from silver card stock and one star from navy blue card stock at 4-inch setting. In the same manner, cut three stars from white card stock and one star from silver card stock at 1½-inch setting. In the same manner, cut one star from navy blue card stock at 1-inch setting.

Skill Level
Easy

Materials
- Cricut Expression machine
- Cartridge: Wild Card (#29-0591)
- Cuttlebug machine
- Embossing folder of your choice
- Card stock: white, navy blue, silver
- Silver printed paper
- 9 inches 1½-inch-wide metallic silver ribbon
- Adhesive foam dots
- Paper adhesive

Wrap silver ribbon over score line of menorah card; secure ends to back of card. Adhere card at a slant to left side of layout as shown. Cut a 6¾ x 3¾-inch rectangle from silver card stock; adhere centered to top of menorah card.

Using Cuttlebug machine and embossing folder, emboss a 6¼ x 3¼-inch rectangle of white card stock. Adhere to center of silver rectangle. Adhere photo to white rectangle.

Using foam dots, attach silver "Hanukkah" to upper right section of silver ribbon. In the same manner, attach white "Hanukkah" overlapping silver "Hanukkah" as shown.

Adhere Stars of David to silver printed paper around menorah card as desired. ●

Source: Cricut machine and cartridge, Cuttlebug machine and embossing folder from Provo Craft.

The TREE Hunt

Recall the fun and excitement of a favorite holiday tradition on this easy-to-create layout.

Design by **Summer Fullerton**

Skill Level
Easy

Materials
- Cricut Expression machine
- Cartridge:
  Winter Woodland (#29-1046)
- Card stock: white, pink, brown
- Printed papers: green snowflake, pink, dark pink, brown
- Black fine-tip marker
- Pink buttons: 2 small, 2 medium, 2 large
- Self-adhesive brown pearl
- Glitter glue
- Adhesive foam squares
- Paper adhesive

Project note: When selecting fonts on cartridges with only images on overlay keypad, refer to cartridge handbook to find font key placements.

Use one 12 x 12-inch sheet of green printed paper as layout base.

Using Winter Woodland cartridge and pink card stock, cut 1½-inch "the TREE hunt." Select Font feature and press "<shift lock>," "<t>," "<r>," "<e>" and "<e>." Release "<shift lock>" and press "<t>," "<h>," "<e>," "<h>," "<u>," "<n>" and "<t>."

Cut 4-inch trees from two pink printed papers and pink card stock by using Blackout/Shadow feature; press "<shift>" and "<Trees>." Cut a 4-inch tree top from white card stock using Layers feature; press "<Trees>."

Cut a 1½-inch squirrel from brown printed paper and brown card stock by pressing "<squirrel>."

Adhere "the TREE hunt" to top of page; accent with layered buttons.

Decorate tree tops with glitter glue. Select one tree of each printed paper and pink card stock; adhere tree tops to three selected trees. Adhere trees to layout as shown, using foam squares on one.

Cut tail off card-stock squirrel; adhere to printed paper squirrel. Adhere to page as shown; attach pearl as eye. Adhere photos to layout as represented by white photo rectangles. ●

Sources: Card stock from Bazzill Basics Paper Inc.; printed papers from BasicGrey, Jillibean Soup and K&Company; Cricut machine and cartridge from Provo Craft.

Season's Greetings

Enjoy a sleigh ride, presents and happy memories of Christmas!

Design by **Joy Tracey**

Use two 12 x 12-inch sheets of Holly Berry paper as layout base.

Cut two 12 x 5-inch rectangles of 'Tis the Season paper. Adhere a 12 x 4½-inch rectangle of Mistletoe paper to each Tis the Season rectangle. Adhere layered rectangles to each layout page as shown.

Cut three 3¾ x 5¾-inch rectangles from Mistletoe papers. Adhere to red card stock as shown; trim small borders. Adhere layered rectangles to right page as shown.

Using Songbird cartridge and Mistletoe paper, cut a 5½-inch photo mat by pressing "<Frame2>." In the same manner, cut bottom layer for mat from red printed paper, selecting Shadow feature first.

Using the Winter Woodland cartridge and black card stock, cut a 2½-inch Season's Greetings base by pressing "<shift>" and "<SeasGrtg>." In the same manner, cut next layer from cream glitter card stock by selecting Shadow feature first. Cut next 2½-inch layer from red glitter card stock by pressing "<SeasGrtg>." Repeat cut using green glitter card stock. Cut final layer from green glitter card stock by selecting Layers feature; press "<SeasGrtg>." Repeat cut using red card stock, pressing "<shift>" first.

Skill Level
Intermediate

Materials
- Cricut Expression machine
- Cartridges:
  Winter Woodland (#29-1046),
  Songbird (#2000063),
  Sweet Treats (#29-1557)
- Card stock: black, gold, cream
- Glitter card stock: red, green, white, cream
- Double-sided printed papers: St. Nick Holly Berry, St. Nick Mistletoe, 'Tis the Season,
- Printed papers: red sparkle spirals, green/red, red, green/silver metallic, red/white dot
- Olive green ink pad
- Stamps: journaling lines, Christmas tree
- Black fine-tip pen
- Red button
- 3 inches ⅝-inch-wide olive green satin ribbon
- White twine
- Adhesive foam dots
- Paper adhesive

Cut a 4-inch sleigh from gold card stock by pressing "<Sleigh>." At same setting, cut top layer from red printed paper by pressing "<shift>" first. In the same manner, cut base layer from black card stock by selecting Shadow feature; press "<Sleigh>." Cut top scalloped layer from white glitter card stock by selecting Layers feature; press "<Sleigh>." Repeat cut using green glitter card stock. Cut final layer from red glitter card stock by selecting Layers feature; press "<shift>" and "<Sleigh>."

Cut a 2½-inch holly from red/white dot paper by pressing "<Holly>." In the same manner, cut background from black card stock by selecting Shadow/Blackout feature first. Cut holly leaves from green glitter card stock by pressing "<shift>" and "<Holly>." Repeat last cut.

Cut a 3½-inch tag from red printed paper by selecting Tag feature, pressing "<bldg3>." Repeat cut with a 3¼-inch setting using cream card stock.

Using Sweet Treats cartridge and red sparkle spirals paper, cut a 2½-inch present by pressing "<present1>." In the same manner, cut present top from white glitter card stock by pressing "<shift>" first. Cut a 2½-inch bow from green/silver metallic paper by selecting Layers feature; press "<present1>."

Cut a 2½-inch second present from green/silver metallic paper by pressing "<present2>." In the same manner, cut bow from red sparkle spirals paper by pressing "<shift>" first. Cut center of bow from white glitter card stock by selecting Layers feature; press "<present2>."

Adhere photo mat layers together. Adhere to left page as shown.

Adhere gold Season's Greetings layer to black base. Adhere red and green glitter layers as shown. Using foam squares, attach to left page as shown.

Adhere gold layer of deer to black layer. Using fine-tip pen, draw details onto deer. Adhere to left page as shown.

Assemble and adhere sleigh preset layers. Adhere presents to sleigh as shown. Adhere layered sleigh next to deer on layout.

Assemble and adhere holly layers. Using foam squares, attach to upper left corner of right page.

Stamp journaling lines and Christmas tree onto white tag, adhere to red tag. Adhere to right page as shown.

String button with white twine; tie bow. Adhere button and ribbon to layered tag as shown. ●

Sources: Card stock from Core'dinations; glitter card stock from Die Cuts With A View; double-sided printed papers from Bo-Bunny Press; printed papers from Reminisce; and Cricut machine and cartridges from Provo Craft.

Joyful Holiday

Showcase the beauty of winter and the joys of the holidays with this fun-to-create layout.

Design by **Melanie Brown**

Skill Level
Intermediate

Materials
- Cricut Expression machine
- Cartridges:
  Straight from the Nest (#2000190),
  Create a Critter (#2000099)
- Card stock: white, dark brown, light brown, black, red
- Soup Staples double-sided printed papers: Green Sugar, Red Sugar, Orange Sugar, Dark Brown Sugar, Light Blue Sugar
- Ink pads: brown, blue
- Round white glitter brad
- 3 (16-inch) lengths ⅜-inch-wide green/white dot satin ribbon
- Clear dimensional gloss medium
- Adhesive foam squares
- Paper adhesive

Use two 12 x 12-inch sheets of white card stock as layout base; ink edges blue. Cut two 11½ x 11¼-inch rectangles of Light Blue Sugar paper; adhere to layout base as shown.

Using Straight from the Nest cartridge and Orange Sugar paper, cut two 2-inch scalloped borders by selecting border feature and pressing "<Cake>."

Using Create a Critter cartridge and brown card stock, cut a 4¼-inch tree by selecting Accessory feature and pressing "<Raccoon>." Repeat. Cut a 4¼-inch top layer for tree from Green Sugar paper by selecting Accessory feature. Press "<Shift>" and "<Raccoon>." Repeat.

Cut a 2-inch "Joy" title from Red Sugar paper by selecting Phrase feature and pressing "<Reindeer>." Cut a 2-inch "Joy" layer from Green Sugar paper by selecting Phrase feature; press "<Shift>" and "<Reindeer>."

Cut a 3¾-inch reindeer base from dark brown card stock by selecting Layer 1 feature and pressing "<Reindeer>." Cut a 3¾-inch second layer of reindeer from light brown card stock by selecting Layer 2 feature and pressing "<Reindeer>." Cut a 3¾-inch scarf and nose layer for reindeer from red card stock by selecting Layer 3 feature; press "<Reindeer>."

Cut a 3¼-inch house from Dark Brown Sugar paper by selecting Accessory feature and pressing "<Pig>." Cut a 3¼-inch top layer for house from light brown card stock by selecting Accessory feature; press "<Shift>" and "<Pig>."

Cut an 1½-inch light base from black card stock by selecting Shadow feature; press "<Shift>" and "<Reindeer>." Cut a 1½-inch first layer for lights from Green Sugar paper by selecting Layer 1 feature. Press "<Shift>" and "<Reindeer>." Repeat with Orange Sugar and Red Sugar papers.

Adhere orange scalloped borders to each layout page as shown.

Cut three 6½ x 4½-inch rectangles of Red Sugar paper. Cut three 6⅛ x 4⅛-inch rectangles of white card stock; adhere to red rectangles. Tie a 16-inch length of ribbon around each rectangle as shown; tie bows. Referring to photo, adhere layered rectangles to pages.

Layer green "Joy" over red "Joy." Use dimensional gloss medium in middle of "o." Once dry, use foam squares to attach word to top right of layout below scallop border.

Ink edges of green tree layers brown. Assemble trees together; adhere trees on left and right lower sides of layout pages.

Tear two strips of white card stock for snow border; ink torn edges blue. Adhere to bottoms of Light Blue Sugar rectangles, overlapping tree trunks as shown.

Ink edges of light brown layer of reindeer brown. Assemble reindeer as shown. Using foam squares, attach to layout over snow border.

Using brown ink, ink edges of roof and door of house; assemble house. Attach brad for door knob.

Adhere lights to light base. Detail lights using dimensional gloss medium. When dry, adhere light strand to roof of house. Using foam squares, attach layered house to right page of layout over snow border as shown. ●

Sources: Printed papers from Jillibean Soup; clear dimensional gloss medium from Plaid Enterprises Inc.; Cricut machine and cartridges from Provo Craft.

Buyer's Guide

American Crafts Inc.
(801) 226-0747
www.americancrafts.com

BasicGrey
(801) 544-1116
www.basicgrey.com

Bazzill Basics Paper Inc.
(800) 560-1610
www.bazzillbasics.com

Bo-Bunny Press
(801) 771-4010
www.bobunny.com

Clearsnap Inc.
(888) 448-4862
www.clearsnap.com

Close To My Heart
www.closetomyheart.com

Core'dinations
www.coredinations.com

Die Cuts With A View
(801) 224-6766
www.diecutswithaview.com

Doodlebug Design Inc.
www.doodlebugdesign.homestead.com

Fiskars
(866) 348-5661
www.fiskarscrafts.com

Hampton Art
(800) 981-5169
www.hamptonart.com

Heidi Swapp/Advantus
(904) 482-0092
www.heidiswapp.com

Hero Arts
www.heroarts.com

Jenni Bowlin Studio
www.jennibowlin.com

Jillibean Soup
(888) 212-1177
www.jillibean-soup.com

K&Company
(800) 794-5866
www.kandcompany.com

Making Memories
(800) 286-5263
www.makingmemories.com

Martha Stewart Crafts
www.marthastewartcrafts.com

My Mind's Eye
(800) 665-5116
www.mymindseye.com

October Afternoon
(866) 513-5553
www.octoberafternoon.com

Pebbles Inc.
(800) 438-8153
www.pebblesinc.com

Pink Paislee
(816) 729-6124
www.pinkpaislee.com

Plaid Enterprises Inc.
(800) 842-4197
www.plaidonline.com

Provo Craft
(800) 937-7686
www.provocraft.com

Reminisce
www.designbyreminisce.com

Scenic Route Paper Co.
(801) 653-1319
www.scenicroutepaper.com

SEI
(800) 333-3279
www.shopsei.com

Technique Tuesday
www.techniquetuesday.com

Zva Creative
(801) 243-9281
www.zvacreative.com

The Buyer's Guide listings are provided as a service to our readers and should not be considered an endorsement from this publication.